E
169.12   Sack
.S22   The man-eating
1973   machine

Date Due

11/74			

D1248965

The Man-Eating Machine

The

Man-Eating Machine

JOHN SACK

Farrar, Straus and Giroux

NEW YORK

About half of this book first appeared in *Esquire*
in much different form. The author is deeply
grateful to Harold Hayes and Don Erickson of *Esquire*
for their invaluable help.

for Harold Hayes

*Is the elimination
of man so unavoidably necessary?
Certainly!*

JACQUES ELLUL

D o not believe it when newspapers say, THE WAR'S
OVER. A war of rich against poor, of white against yellow
—no, Vietnam was another front in the armageddon of
the machine against man, and the most infamous of its
atrocities was a small exaggeration of what happens every
day in the mill wheels of Main street. So like a machine
is our society that we ourselves are a quite unwelcome intrusion and—by inches, usually, or with dispatch, occa-
sionally—we must be eliminated whether we're in Manhattan or Mylai. As one philosopher said of our thing in
Vietnam, "Who did it? Our whole way of life did it."

That is the point of the stories here. A white and
a Negro soldier in combat clothes in the combat area, a
Negro and a white veteran in three-piece suits in Manhattan—the four stories in this book really happened. The
names, the quotations, the thoughts—everything here is
the concentrate of some three thousand pages of handwrit-
ten notes. Demirgian served in C Company of the
2d Battalion of the 2d Infantry, in the 3d Brigade of
the 1st Division, and the attack occurred at Hoanhut,
in Binhduong Province, on November 15, 1965. Melvin

worked at Benton & Bowles, 666 Fifth Avenue, New York, New York, and his meeting with the vice-president was on May 19, 1969. Thompson served in D Company of the 1st Battalion of the 58th Infantry, in the 197th Infantry Brigade, and the fire occurred at Taback's Grocery, in Baltimore, Maryland, on April 9, 1968. Calley stayed at Delmonico's Hotel, 502 Park Avenue, New York, New York, and his testimony about the irrigation ditch was on February 23, 1971.

CONTENTS

1 / VAROUJAN   3

2 /   35

3 / BOB   43

4 /   95

5 / VANTEE   103

6 /   141

7 / BILL   149

The Man-Eating Machine

I / VAROUJAN

Ninety-nine bottles of beer on the wall, ninety-nine bottles of beer. If one of those bottles should happen to fall, ninety-eight bottles of beer on the wall. Ninety-eight bottles of—

Time was a row of old brown bottles toppling down. Of old crystal balls cracking apart, and Demirgian, the three hundreds, two hundreds, one hundreds over, the days strewn behind him like broken glass, a staleness about them, a sickening smell—a normal young man, Demirgian had just eighty-eight days in Vietnam ahead. C-ration cans, cigarettes, iron, brass, lead, Vietnam had another eighty-eight days of Demirgian, too. His rank specialist, his specialty rifle, his duty shooting at communists with it, Demirgian's dream, Demirgian's *raison d'être* was to kill himself one. He could see it: *Charlie tries to creep up on me,* Demirgian mused, *Charlie tries that and I'll lie here—yeah, I'll let him get ten meters from me. Yeah, and I'll have a hand grenade and I'll pull the pin—Charlie, you've had it! And kkk, and I'll let the handle go and I'll one—! two—! and I'll throw it!* Thumb on the bottom, fingers on top, a lazy little catlike windup, the pitch—he would throw the grenade like a baseball, a rock, he had practiced that in Newton, Massachusetts, the city where he had grown up. *"Foreigner,"* the kids had cried at Demirgian, *"Camel-chaser,"* the Irish would say, and Demirgian, age twelve, his body behind a cardboard carton with the color of dead lawns and a dry-spell smell, his eyes at two tiny fiber-filled holes—Demirgian had thrown pudding stone at the Irish, that is how he would throw his grenade at that communist if the stars in their slowly meandering courses should offer him—*at last*—one of his unseen enemies. A year in Vietnam, a year minus eighty-eight days and Demirgian had still never killed, wounded, scratched, or stuck out a tongue at—still never seen a VC to have himself at. Good luck, Demirgian.

Tonight, Demirgian lay in his combat clothes: helmet, his damp shirt and trousers, canvas boots, and Demirgian had a wet black rifle on the soil beside him as his fingertips made a Kool-Aid. As quietly as a caterpillar chews, he tore the little packet apart, and as quietly as a dandelion loses its fluff he let some purple powder into his Army canteen. The stars above, the earth below stayed silent as Demirgian tilted the rubber canteen to the left—right—left—right—with a pendulum's slow periodicity. A minute, and Demirgian took a quiet sip. And then came alive, Demirgian was in the grape-juice generation now. He buried the torn paper quietly in Vietnam's soil.

The time was about ten-thirty. It shouldn't be thought that on Army ambushes (for Demirgian's squad was

on ambush assignment tonight: to lie in that total darkness, if anyone comes it's a communist, shoot him)—
it shouldn't be thought that the GIs were panthers ready
to leap, their legs up under them, their eyes all alert:
ridiculous. The essence of ambushes was that nothing—
nothing—happened, nowhere but in the grave did the
hours pass by a mass of human substance so stubbornly
true to its configuration of one hour earlier, nobody in
an American ambush did a damn cotton-picking thing,
the hours between sunset and sunrise hung like a ham-
mock between two willow trees, once in a hundred times
did a star-crossed communist happen by. Demirgian, a
year of these uninteresting affairs and he hadn't ambushed
one living breathing soul. He had just waited, he had
scratched at where the mosquitoes bit, in his feet he had
pins and needles: therefore, he had wiggled his toes, he
had given himself to little insidious itches, the nibbles of
little millions of imaginary ants, he had breathed in—out
—in—out—he had carefully not neglected to breathe, the
earth, like a big brown blotter, had sopped up his *élan
vital,* his muscle tone, his temperature, his blood, at dawn
he had lifted himself like a heavy tarpaulin and carried
himself to the company camp. It was three meals a day,
pink pills on Sunday, payday on the thirtieth—*monoto-
nous.*

It was eleven o'clock now. A boy on Demirgian's
ambush snored. Another said, "Sergeant? I have a headache."

"You have a headache?"

"You have an aspirin?"

"I have a Darvon."

"Please."

It's crazy, Demirgian thought. Inside of Demirgian's rifle was a full hundred thousand millionth of one percent of the year's gross national product. A bullet, it had been mined in Colorado, roasted, smelted, refined, and transported to Connecticut. And splash! at the bullet factory, it had been dropped in a melting pot to emanate as a wire: coiling it, oiling it, the great machine sent it along. The machine was gargantuan, gears all like wagon wheels, connecting rods all in the motions of heavy animal love. And chop! and chop! the wire was in bullet sizes, the bullets were on a slippery slide: were the sleighs on a snowy hillside, jingle all the way. Now careful of the powder, girls and boys! No smoking, please, as birdlike ladies in glasses of plastic took the black powder, the bullets, the brass, as forty-nine at a time were made in the U.S.A. And a thousand wheels went around and around! And the air's on edge in that factory sound! And boxes of bullets abound on the ground! And—

Click. Clack. Every day, Demirgian put an American bullet into his mean-looking rifle. A power uncalled upon, an American eagle asleep, there in its little lair the bullet would stay, a bullet was an unessential item in a war where the enemy's awol. It was crazy, indeed: so much sweat and so few results from it. The miners in Colorado with lead-covered lungs, the truckers with the EXPLOSIVES behind them, the men in Connecticut in iron shoes so they wouldn't break their toes, the women in plastic glasses so they wouldn't go blind, accidentally, the supers, inspectors, directors, the President too—Americans by the millions had willingly given up life, liberty, and the pursuit of everything else to put that bullet into Demirgian's barrel. And behind it, Demirgian: he was there through the self-sacrifice of farmers, millers, bakers, of salt, soda, calcium propionate manufacturers, of sailors, shipmasters, longshoremen, of millions more for his C-ration bread alone. In fact, every bloomin' soul in Demirgian's acquaintance was a wheel in that green machine, the Army—

Except. One's sorry to say this: except for the Vietnamese, the Vietnamese were the broken link and it was their fault that the green machine didn't go. If those people were to get with it, Demirgian just could ambush, ambush, and ambush—imagine, a radio telephone rings and Demirgian says, "Demirgian."

"My name is Ho," a rice farmer says in the language that he has thoughtfully gone to Berlitz for. "I live in the house with the light on—I hear VC outside."

"Be right there," Demirgian tells him. Or tells him, "Go to the cellar immediately, and I'll call in a TOT attack." Or tells him, "Go to Saigon—" "Singapore—" "Somewhere— I'm sorry, I'll have to nuke it."

"Roger," the Vietnamese answers. "Will do."

If only the Vietnamese fitted in, Demirgian's bullets, Demirgian's bombs, boiling oil, belladonna, axes, tarantulas, pet rattlesnakes, laser rays, lye, Demirgian's man-eating miracle rice—Demirgian's wonderful weapons would work. He just would order the Vietnamese people, "Attention." And dress right dress, and forward march out to ten million rubber rafts. And then three! two! one! in one immense mushroom cloud, the war would be totally over. If those people fitted in, Demirgian now would be home again, uninjured, undead.

It wasn't especially likely. Give a good rubber raft to a Vietnamese and he would sell it for shower shoes for Americans (*Or for the VC,* Demirgian thought)—he would choose to die in his straw house on that ultimate operation. And that being so, Demirgian had nothing to do except sit in "ambushes" every night to look at bananas bloom and to listen to bullets rust. But coming in in the morning, bang! he would shoot at a C-ration can. And bang! he would shoot at a squealing pig. And bang! he would get a chicken with one of America's accurate bullets. "Demirgian. You character," the other soldiers would grin—the sharp of the shooting gallery, give him a box of Mars bars, give him a cuddly teddy bear. Or better: give him a VC sometime. There were boys in Demirgian's squad who had yes! had killed communists, it had been known to happen sometimes in spite of Vietnam's uncooperative ways. It wasn't unheard of.

EXTRA. EXTRA. GI KILLS ENEMY SOLDIER. *We began elbowing through the bush, our forearms slashed by thorns and our fatigues drenched with sweat. Suddenly—*

Suddenly, *Newsweek* reported, a boy in Demirgian's squad saw a real enemy soldier—*the bullet ripped through the Vietcong's head*. Though his name wasn't spelled right in *Newsweek,* he had been given a hero's due by Demirgian's proud battalion commander, a trip via cargo plane to the China sea, a holiday spree at the beaches: time out, a Coppertone tan, a blanket, sand, a date in a blue bikini, only the brave deserve the fair. Another day, a Red was made dead by the steady machine gun of Demirgian's closest friend, Demirgian's buddy. His holiday over, he had returned with his China-sea suntan to see himself recommended for a bronze star and a "V" for that extraordinary act. But scandalously, the company clerk was a GI who walked as though holding a hula hoop up: a typical clerk, and Demirgian's friends had always made fun by telling him in the tent, toilet, and shower tent, "Gentlemen only," or asking him, "Tuck me in?" The clerk was so wrought up ("Careful," Demirgian's friends would say. "Or he'll hit you with his purse")—so angry that he had thrown the recommendation for a bronze star and a "V" away. But another friend got an Army commendation medal, *Suddenly,* the Army citation said, *the insurgent unit approached. He then opened fire—*

It could happen, Demirgian knew. Day after day, for every fifteen hundred men in Vietnam who didn't kill a VC, statistically there was one who did. And typically got a medal for it, a starred or a striped ribbon, and a citation ending with, "His actions are in the highest traditions of the military service." This, a PFC at Demirgian's headquarters sat up each night to ten-thirty writing. An alumnus of Rutgers, it had occurred to him that shooting a VC was only traditional if a GI approached it with certain *élan.* Accordingly, he had written things like

> *relentless efforts*
> *tenacious adherence*
> *indomitable resolution*
> *unwavering determination*

on a stenographer's pad, to use like tinker toys to make those citations out of. Eschewing the arbitrary, the Rutgers boy bestowed the bronze star for *bravery,* the silver star for *unquestionable valor,* and the DSC for *extraordinary heroism.* It didn't matter: let a GI kill every communist in China or one dumb machine gunner, he didn't get a medal of honor without a citation saying that he had never relented from his determined effort to destroy the enemy and to assist his fallen comrades, unquote.

But Demirgian. A medal, *Who needs it,* Demirgian thought, Demirgian didn't want it, Demirgian was dying to kill those communists with or without it. For someone with no past animus to Asians of any political party, a year on their continent and he was fierce, he had bones like a thing turned black, a thin black liquid ran in his arteries, it baffled some of the newer boys, the reason— that was Demirgian's secret. A bullet, a piece of his bayonet, it didn't make a diff to Demirgian how, a tent peg if it was sharp enough, a shovel, a can of kerosene, a kitchen match and—*bastard, die!* A kick in his genitals,

finger in his eyeballs, stick him in the ashcan—hahaha,
Demirgian thought, a toss of a hand grenade, success!
An explosion, and D would look at him lying dead and
I'll think—Demirgian thought of a pale yellow face, the
mouth like a broken bottle, the starlight on crooked teeth
—*I think I'll be sorry about him. Yeah,* Demirgian
thought. *I'll say, "You poor bastard! You're with a losing
cause. You poor little dumb little dirty—"*

Eleven-thirty. Midnight almost, and the sergeant
for Demirgian's ambush was praying, was saying, *"Padre
nuestro,"* was putting his face to the ground, *"que estás
in los cielos, santificado . . ."*
One click, one kilometer, from the area where the
passing hours went by Demirgian's squad like a trickle
of lukewarm water was Demirgian's company camp, a
Kipling locale: a tight triangular area of Army huts and
holes. And just outside, the Coke stand, as soldiers called
it, was deserted, of course, it was closed until dawn, but
that afternoon as Vietnamese small businessmen stood at
its shaky wooden tables to give soldiers beer and Coke,
to busily pop bottle tops off with rusty openers, to grow
a garden of bottle tops in their fatherland's soil, to over-
charge and to shout at their weary customers not to walk
off with the empties—that day, there had been something
unheard of. Sitting drinking a bottle of Vietnam's for-
maldehyde beer, a GI had sought to fill up the empty
interstices of time by saying one of those phrases whose

endless reiteration passed for conversation at the Coke stand, "Hey, mamasan, VC come tonight?" A catechism, but that afternoon instead of her cackling laugh and her inveterate answer, "VC no come tonight," the Vietnamese in her black wrinkled rayon had scaredly said, "Yes."

Mirabile dictu. It was something to shout about, that a Vietnamese had done something more for the Vietnamese war effort than to just cater it. Money, money, that's what the Coke crowd cared about, the GIs believed. Once, Demirgian had bought himself orange pop, he had paid out a fifty-piaster bill, the lady had pushed it into her dress, and Demirgian had said politely, "Change?" At that, the lady had started to shriek: to *shriek* in the half-hysterical *ow*'s of a dog when there's someone on its tail, to shriek at Demirgian and the echoing acres that fifty piasters—fifty cents—was a fair market price for a bottle of pop in Asia. It was morning, and Demirgian was used to the silence of the ambush that he had been lying on all that night to enable the shrieking lady to engage in free enterprise. It rankled that he had risked life and limb for a race of such ingrates as to challenge, in shrieks, even his right to renew himself with a bottle of soda without paying them ten times the wholesale price. He felt if a GI had—and a GI *had*—to twist the Vietnamese lady's arm, to give her a quick karate chop at the base of her cervical spine, or simply to shoot a few holes in her damn shrieking skull to get some cooperation, that he was just angry enough to do it. A bottle of Crush:

A guy's gotta eat, Demirgian thought, the Army moved on its stomach.

It wasn't only the Coke-stand crowd. It was everywhere, the Vietnamese way of not doing anything as a man ought to. Mad dogs and Vietnamese went out in the sun although only the Vietnamese went wearing black, *It's hotter that way,* Demirgian thought. A headache: to treat it, a Vietnamese had kept trying to pinch it, Demirgian saw. In a war where the GIs took orders in English, the Vietnamese didn't even try to: FATAL, it said on a Brasso bottle, but as Demirgian watched her a Vietnamese used it for tooth polish once, *It can kill her! She's stupid,* Demirgian thought. And what happened when an American spoke with the aye-aye's cry of a Vietnamese? Always this:

"VC adai?" Where are the VC?

"Khong biet," I don't know.

"VC adai!" Where are the VC!

"Khong biet," I don't know.

It just exasperated everyone. A wooden shoe in the wheelworks: that's what the Vietnamese were, the wrench in the war machine, the hitch, the fatal insertion of human uncertainty into the System. *These people,* the GIs just could do zero about them. A mission impossible was to reform them, to rid those people of errors, inefficiencies, improprieties, impurities—*dirt,* to just clean them up. The company tried: it had honestly tried, it had scrubbed at those bodies, hearts, and minds, it had almost become a Society for the Suppression of Savage Customs, Kurtz's society in Conrad. In one little village, a GI who wanted to cleanse them of *everything* and of its objective correlative, dirt—a GI had taken his Lifebuoy out. He had pantomimed with it: had magically passed it up and down while telling the Vietnamese children, "Washee washee. Washee," the GI concluded, and he had given his great unwashed audience the Lifebuoy bar. And would you believe it? The children ate it—phooie, a GI could just say, "Impossible. Impossible people."

It wasn't racism, though. The black hair, the almond eyes, the meadow-mushroom noses: the *yellow,* the GIs didn't dislike it, Korean soldiers, Philippine nurses, Chinese prostitutes had it and still fitted in. Heads erect, GIs —*officers*—would take a Thai to the officers club in Bangkok, "I'm sorry, sir. You can't take a prostitute in." "What?" "You can't take a prostitute in." "What? Are you calling my wife a prostitute?" And even the Vietnamese, the Vietnamese could become yellower than the canaries and be a GI's very best friends if they wouldn't be so—*Vietnamese,* if they would work for America, if they would talk in English, if they would telephone us or set lanterns out, *The commies are coming,* one if by land, two if by sampan, if they would simply adjust to a Great Society in Asia. If they would adapt to corps, corporations, to going to work every morning with a tan attaché case—

"Hey, mamasan," the GI had asked. "VC come tonight?"

"Yes."

"You say VC come tonight?"

"Yes."

"You fulla bullshit."

No one there at the Coke stand believed her. A loud little woman, her mouth the size of a mouse hole, her teeth the color of cockroaches—the GIs had just dismissed her. No one even reported her—the Captain hears, he gets nervous in the service, he puts everyone on alert, and we never sleep, the GIs all reasoned. And that was why at eleven-thirty the GIs were mostly asleep in their camouflage while a VC battalion lay in the dark in range of Demirgian's rifle. Any minute, it would attack.

WHAT DID YOU DO IN THE WAR, DADDY-O? *Five seconds. Four seconds. Three seconds. Two seconds. One—* A soldier in a well-starched uniform kept a close eye on a wall clock that was as large as the harvest moon, and at *zero* he tapped on a green button—go! A circle of gray steel rotated, acetate issued from it, this interrupted the quanta discriminately, electrons arose, a shower of electromagnetism fell on Vietnam like the monsoon rain: not a grain of rice escaped it. On earth, at a thousand receptors it was reconstituted into the phosphorus images of Batman and Robin. Holy von Clausewitz, it's the Armed Forces Television Network! Zow!

But they didn't have TV at Demirgian's dark ambush area, and Demirgian was bored—was bored. To be sure, reality gave him a whole lot to listen to: *ooooo,* artillery going over, its dull sound on the ground, mortars, machine guns, he had some things to look at: the yellow sky, the yellow from the yellow flares, the sky falling down like a falling tent. A real *son et lumière* that he sat through without curiosity, things in the night weren't new to Demirgian, war was war. But the sergeant who prayed in Spanish was told through the warm rubber telephone of his radio that the company camp was being attacked by two or three hundred communists.

"We been cut off," the sergeant said to the radio operator beside him. "Is no way that we can penetrate back. We—"

"How about the company?" As the radio operator knew, if the company fell the squad would too.

"They are fighting like good ones," the sergeant replied. "We have to stay sweat them out. *So nobody fire,"* he concluded. One little rifle sound, one little ray of red-orange light, one little grenade and the VC in the dark middle distance, advancing, retreating, getting their pep talks, go give 'em hell, comrade, the VC would know of their whereabouts: there wouldn't be a GI alive. *Nobody fire:* a life-and-death strategy, and to impart it the sergeant said he would crawl the ten, twenty, thirty meters to the invisible boys on the left, the radio operator should crawl to the right: to Demirgian.

Thus, at about midnight, the radio operator, a good-looking guy, a newcomer there, a Negro, was doing what he had never done on these ambushes: moving. His chest in the earth, his knees like the claws of crabs, the pebbles going by his stomach, the *ooooo*'s going over him, as the boy crawled he asked himself, *Why am I doing this?* It was a madman's errand, really. To ask of Demirgian to abandon his heart's desire and to arrest his itchy finger no matter how many communists passed—this was an act of saintly restraint that a colonel couldn't urge on that hellcat, easier tell the rattlesnake to ignore the rat. Moreover, the order *don't shoot* couldn't even get to Demirgian till the boy had come within earshot—and rifle shot, it couldn't be delivered until his crawling form was a target to Demirgian's wide-open eyes. *Now what's with Demirgian?* the boy used to ask himself, a GI is taught to fire at the communist areas, pick up the brass, give me a piece of your fruitcake, thanks—a job is a job, don't have to get ferocious about it. But Demirgian! What was Demirgian after, get a holiday at the China sea? Get a medal for killing a communist? Get a souvenir: a Russian watch or some raggedy wet piasters to buy orange pop at the Coke stand with? Demirgian was a holy terror, the radio operator knew—was it psychological, perhaps? Had the Irish who called him a camel-chaser sublimated to Asians? Or did Demirgian feel inferior, a year in Vietnam in the wilds and woolies and he still wasn't a man, he didn't have a scalp although others did? Or simply, did Demirgian want to be written up in *Newsweek,* that's all? "His forearms were being slashed by thorns . . ." Often, the boy had wondered what was Demirgian bugged by, never, though, had he guessed at Demirgian's secret. He had told himself, *Well, Demirgian's an Armenian, that's why.* He had seen television about the Gurkhas once, the Gurkhas all swinging swords at a living breathing ox, a splash, a bucket of blood, an ox head lay on the ground like a rotten melon: a fierce race of people, obviously, and Demirgian had Armenian ancestors, Demirgian's family came from the Gurkha regions. *That's why,* the radio operator said—mistakenly.

He had crawled to ten meters of Demirgian: close enough, and he whispered what he knew would identify him as a bona fide friend, not a VC. The radio operator whispered, "Demirgian!"

He heard Demirgian answer, "Yeah?"

He whispered again, "Don't fire. No matter what," he then crawled to where he had started from, and he opened a cold can of C-rations. His favorite C-rat was turkey loaf: it was everyone's, it disappeared fast and he was making do with boneless chicken tonight, at least it wasn't the Spam ham and lima beans: *ugh,* a little wet cylinder, a cattle lick. With his GI can opener, he fell experiencedly on that chicken can, the opener going as silently as a knitting needle, the red tracers making slaps as they passed above him. The skies were as yellow as Mars's, in the distances yellow smoke rose, at every horizon heaven and earth seemed to have jarred apart, the yellow bowl of heaven rocked on the dark brown earth, the world, it seemed, was against the rocks, it was breaking up.

"What are you doing?"

"Sergeant," the radio operator whispered, "when I'm hungry I eat." He buried his empty can and he quietly split the circumference of a fruit cocktail, thinking, *I need vanilla ice cream—mm,* exactly as mother made it. The noises continued, *ooooo.* For his midnight crawl, there would be more desserts for the boy, the Rutgers alumnus would give him a commendation medal with a "V" for valor and a citation saying, "His actions are in the finest traditions—"

Demirgian. As for Demirgian, the infantryman *terrible* gave a good minute's thought to those whispered words, "Don't fire. No matter what." He asked himself, *What's to fire at?* Nothing in the night's sound and fury seemed special to this survivor of three hundred similar ones, the country was a shooting gallery after dark, it wasn't somewhere for old men, women, and children, but it wasn't new to Demirgian. Old soldier Demirgian forgot it. At twelve, his long boring hours of guard duty ended, and rolling over he whispered, "Hey, sergeant. Wake up." And then as the skies issued sounds like a house of a thousand shutters in a September storm, Demirgian rolled on his shoulder blades and Demirgian fell asleep.

Meanwhile—at Demirgian's camp, the VC had now broken through. A corner of that black triangle was VC-held: a bunker, inside it a couple of Coke bottles, bottle caps, the colorful crumbs of fruitcake, pound cake in a C-ration can, a can that was empty, lids, a couple of comic books, Playmates, mosquito repellent, cigarettes, the empty brass of Demirgian's bullets—that, and some communist soldiers too. But then came the reinforcements, hurrah! The men, the weapons, the bullets made in Connecticut by sweet old ladies in plastic shoes—the wherewithals came in a tank except *bang,* the VC now ambushed it. From out of the tank wreck a tank soldier crawled. A lieutenant, his clothes were in terrible shreds, one of his legs wasn't there, he didn't have one of his arms, instead of his genitals there was a bleeding hole, the phosphorus was in his eyeballs, they were like glowing charcoals—they were like orange "exit" bulbs. All night, he would crawl on the scorching steel, at dawn he would fly to Washington to recuperate—

"Hey, sergeant. Wake up," Demirgian had just whispered.

The sergeant was on his back almost asleep when Demirgian's tiny whisper changed him to almost awake. Nor did the Negro sergeant roll to the prone position, roll to his stomach. The silhouette of a hip, a shoulder going over, an arm—anything, he believed, was enough to tell whoever was doing the shooting here of his presence here, and he stayed flat on his back during guard. The secret of his survival: inconspicuousness.

He looked at the stars. Years ago, he had observed that the stars aren't like the Canada geese, the stars aren't shoving ahead or slipping behind, the star patterns that he could see in a Carolina sky lasted for hours—for years, and in Vietnam he was pleased to see that these relationships still held. He looked at these familiar faces as he was standing guard—was lying on guard, the prism, the rocking chair, the cup and the saucer, these are what he had called his precious constellations. Low in that friendly sky was the "V" of Taurus: to the sergeant part of a spaceship, the nose cone. Orion, at this season, lay on its side, its belt was a bandleader's hat to the sergeant's eyes, its sword was a celluloid visor: the sergeant thought of the braid in its broad figure eights, the sergeant could even see it. The silver whistle, the shiny scepter, the downbeat hard as a hand on a wooden table—*be kind to your web-footed friends*. The sergeant had once led a band himself: at a high school for Negroes he had played drums, the clarinet, the brass and baritone tubas, he didn't play the trombone (it didn't ever solo)—he liked the guitar the best, though. As he lay here tonight, he sang to himself,

> *He took a hundred pounds of clay*
> *And he said, Hey listen!*
> *I'm goin' to fix this world today*
> *Because I know what's missin'!*

A pretty song: it reminded him of his wife in North Carolina.

Being in Vietnam made the sergeant sing, a melody held the minutes together as simply twiddling his fingers didn't, time was as thin as skimmed milk if he didn't fill it with well-remembered songs. Demirgian he didn't

understand at all, Demirgian for whom elephant grass
made the senses quicken, the eyes become livelier than a
chirping bird's, the life forces flow, Demirgian who
looked for destructible communists even as the sergeant
tried to keep away acedia by singing, *I can't get no sa . . .
tisfaction.* "Demirgian. Now take it easy," he often had to
preach patience to Demirgian as the disappointed soldier
shot at the pigeons and people's chickens after a day of not
shooting communists. Demirgian's mysterious vendetta
wasn't—well, it wasn't vendetta, the sergeant knew. Not a
boy in Demirgian's whole platoon had been killed by the
communists since the first days of Demirgian's tour. Acci-
dents happen, but Demirgian couldn't fault the communists for "I didn't know it was loaded" behavior, this the
sergeant appreciated. One of Demirgian's late-lamented
friends had been scratching his head with a .45 when he
idiotically pulled the trigger, another who didn't have a
"church key" to open a Crush had tried unintelligently
with a 50-caliber bullet, another had used gasoline to burn
up what's underneath latrines and oh! was burned to
death like a Buddhist, it wasn't the Bolsheviks this. Seven
whole boys (a lieutenant even) had shot themselves in
this or that anatomical organ in one embarrassing week,
the fault was their own and Demirgian wasn't out for re-
venge, obviously—his ferocity wasn't due to it. *Must be,
Demirgian had a brother killed,* the sergeant had told
himself: untrue. Demirgian the fire-eating soldier, a mys-
tery to that newcomer beside him.

"*I love you,*" the sergeant was thinking now.

"No no!"

"I love you. You are more to me than anything in the whole world," the line was Lord Darlington's in *Lady Windermere's Fan.* Who could guess as the sergeant lay on his backbone, as the *ooooo*'s passed over him, and as time condensed from the night air to settle around him as damp as a heavy dew—that the Negro sergeant had played the Darlington part in his segregated school, an ascot on, a pearl stickpin, the hints of his acting teacher firm in his senses: *rawther* instead of *rather,* cup in the right hand and saucer left. The line the sergeant liked best was "Excuse me, you fellows. I have to write a few letters." He had allotted it many reprises, if his open mouth wasn't full of the proper sentence he had simply said, "Excuse me, you fellows . . ." And exited off.

Uh-oh. A squad of VC was quietly coming—the sergeant hadn't eyes in his helmet and he didn't see it. And Demirgian—Demirgian was fast asleep.

IF YOU'VE 'EARD THE EAST A-CALLIN', *No! You won't 'eed nothin' else, But them spicy garlic smells, An' the sunshine an' the palm-trees an' the tinkly temple-bells.*

A vision of sugarplums danced in Demirgian, the sleeping soldier, months ago he had been in Bangkok and there wasn't a night that he didn't dream of his respite from war in that fabulous city—Bangkok! Three hours out of Saigon's impossible airport, ten thousand planes, the planes in the treetops, almost, the planes on each other's shoulders like at automobile graveyards, the noise, the inconsiderateness, the Vietnamese people—three hours after this, and Demirgian had been dining out, a candle, a silver setting, a low teak table reposing like a lion on a purple rug, a picture window, a curtain of tissue-paper flowers: little moths, and through it a garden, the wind in the palm trees, a star. The scene shone, and some music as soft as water over a bed of pebbles came to Demirgian from—Demirgian didn't know. It seemed that the air atoms tapped one another like cat bells in Bangkok—a real revelation, he hadn't known that the Orient offered more to its visitors than the smell of sewage in streets. In this restaurant, girls in silk hostess gowns came to Demirgian crawling, carrying wine or water, smiling, apologizing for being uninvited, saying, "Forgive me for saying so, except—" the flowers, the petals were a carved chestnut, enjoy them. As she crawled to Demirgian, one of these fairies gave him a silver silk bag of perfume, whispering thank you—*thank you.* Never before in Asia had Demirgian heard the words *thank you,* even the loud little children that he gave chewing gum to had never said *"cam on"* in Vietnamese, but had shoved out their other hand. Bangkok had just enchanted him, it didn't smell of deteriorated fish, it had cars, traffic lights, center stripes, it seemed that the people of Bangkok *cared,* the barbers— the barbers had worn white doctors' robes as they shaved the fluff on Demirgian's eyelids and inside his ear canals, squirting in water afterwards, what a wonderful place!

24

Demirgian said to some friends, "If they had a war here, I'd re-enlist if I could go to Thailand, wouldn't you?"

His friends had said yes. Demirgian was on leave here (the Army called it a rest-and-recreation leave, and it gave every boy a week of it)—Demirgian was in Bangkok with two friends, one was Demirgian's most immediate sergeant, a Botticelli angel with a soft, sweet, watery smile, the other was Demirgian's lieutenant, an officer just out of Fort Benning, Georgia. A real source of humor this—if Demirgian asked, "Do you have a match," the lieutenant would say, "I don't light a cigarette for a private, *private*," lighting it, though, the three laughing, friends in Bermudas and sport shirts. After the wine, the carved chestnuts, the Thais with their fingers like cattails, the music of gentle stringed instruments—after this, the GIs had gone to where women were, the Strip, and the sergeant had fallen in love with one, Keri. From then on, the three were a foursome as Keri showed them the temples of her beloved city: Keri, the friendly lieutenant, Keri's new friend the sweet-smiling sergeant, and Demirgian, Demirgian wittily imitating her, "Now this temple is marble. It was begun in the year nothing, and it wasn't done for a thousand years. The legend is—" the boys laughing and Keri laughing too, Keri biting her lower lip so she wouldn't go beyond the bounds of her etiquette.

On the seventh day, they had visited the zoo, the monkeys swinging like Indian clubs, a black arm, a leg, a tail of each spider monkey twisted around the trapezes, the graceful, surprisingly, giraffes, the elephants like an Egyptian relief, a row of them standing and looking left, a rope on their legs to orient them in that direction, the elephants rocking side to side as slowly as heavy punkahs on hot afternoons, the trunks of these elephants swinging, the ears slowly moving like old shredded regimental flags —it seemed that these monumental elephants had been there through all Asian history, swaying side to side. Over the center elephant was a high golden roof: a temple roof, its millions of little sequins the color of old mustard shone in the Bangkok sun, and Keri had said reverentially, "This is the king's elephant."

"Which is the queen's elephant?" Demirgian asked, and Keri had suddenly turned away. "Aw, doesn't the queen have an elephant?" Demirgian asked, and Keri got rigidly silent.

"You shouldn't make fun of their king and queen," the soft-spoken sergeant said.

"I'm not making fun," Demirgian answered honestly. "Which is the king's giraffe?" He kept saying things so Keri would smile again—Keri didn't, "I wish I were king," Demirgian tried, "so I'd have an elephant," failure, to a Thai there's little to say of their king and queen except hosanna, perhaps. "Hey," Demirgian finally said. "Let's try the dodgem cars," and Demirgian ran from those difficult animals. He was sitting in a little blue car, he was driving it every which way, he was—*crash*—he was crashing it into the natives when the others walked up. "Hey, get yourselves one," Demirgian shouted.

The lieutenant wasn't sure. "I don't think the Thais are as barbaric as us, Demirgian," the lieutenant said, the Thais in the other dodgem cars had, in fact, driven them as gingerly as A & P shopping carts, the Thais had just smiled at each other, tipping their hats, in effect, acting as though they had learner's permits till Demirgian charged, Demirgian in clouds of concrete dust, the terror of the five hundred, the wheels rising, the tires crying, the side of his car always crashing on everyone else's, the metal denting, the shower of sparks, the Thais in their battered chariots laughing and Keri, at last, laughing too, Keri now sitting down because of her laughing so, the sergeant laughing, the lieutenant laughing, "Go gettem, cat! Go gettem," Demirgian laughing triumphantly, the Grand Prix of Bangkok his.

In the evening they ate at the river, the sunset lay on the temple tops and slivers of orange sunset fell in the silver river and drifted by like goldfish, Keri said to the real catfish, "Here, baby. Here," giving the fish little bits of bread to nibble on. That night, Keri slept with the sergeant, washing him, drying him, crying when he said goodbye, when he told her, "I will be back," really meaning it. A little later at Saigon's airport, the Vietnamese pushing, the porters not getting the change right, the dirt, the speaker issuing static and *"Attention all Army personnel,"* the GIs had scarcely landed when they met a boy from their platoon, the lieutenant naturally asking him, "What's new?" Well, in Vietnam it had been another week, the GI said—Demirgian's friend, Demirgian's buddy, had been accidentally shot by the squad sergeant and, well, the platoon sergeant had been killed by Army artillery, idiotically one of our cannon shells fell on his sleeping bag, it was hi-dee-hee in the field artillery and, of course, the first sergeant, he had been saying police up this, police up that, exactly as some clumsy son-of-a-dumbbell stepped on a detonator and as *"police up"* died on the first sergeant's lips the first sergeant died and oh, yes, another company, unintentionally it had been napalmed, twenty or thirty soldiers were in the hospital, another twenty or thirty dead, and—so, it had been a ridiculous week, the GI concluded, a man couldn't deny it. Demirgian left for a hot dog while saying to Keri's sergeant, "Vietnam. The cesspool of the universe."

 ·"Of the universe," the sergeant repeated—he was shaking now. He was still acting strange the next day ("He looked like he was underwater," a GI would testify) —the next afternoon when he got to his quarters: the company camp, a dark canvas tent, a long row of cots, a couple of Vietnamese laundry boys on a cot, sitting, look-ing at dirty photographs of people making love, and say-ing things like "Fucky-fucky," laughing, letting their wide red palates show. "Now damn it! Now wipe those smiles off," the sergeant wanted to say—smiles, nakedness, making love, and a whole lot of life were experiences that a GI has said goodbye to, a GI has cleaned himself and a

Vietnamese should too. Get with it and wipe those smiles off! And that laughter off! And that loafing off! And that— *Move on over, mothers, or I'll move on over you!* And into his rifle the sergeant put a Connecticut bullet, click, clack. "I'm going to do some hunting," the sergeant said.

"I hope you'll do your hunting out yonder," a GI replied.

"I can do my hunting right here," the sergeant said.

And after killing the Vietnamese laundry boys, he was court-martialed, convicted, and sentenced to a life sentence at Leavenworth. "Well, okay. He disliked the Vietnamese—fine," the prosecutor said. "If he wants to hate the Vietnamese—fine. But *killing* is not quite correct."

"Huh?" Demirgian said.

The boys with Demirgian had woken him up around dawn to relate the alarms and excursions while God had his guardian angels over him: how the company camp had been attacked, a corner taken, a tank carried to kingdom come, a tank getting through, *tarantara,* the tide of war turning, communists retreating, company enduring, hurrah! No one in Demirgian's army had been killed by those two or three hundred communists (a GI was shot accidentally, nothing more)—a very great victory for America. By the hard yellow flares, Demirgian now glimpsed some of the forty communist dead, the easy victims of American artillery and American planes, fat fire-breathing planes that the GIs had given the nickname of Puff the Magic Dragon—

Lived by the sea,

the Negro sergeant had thought as the dragon's rain of red tracer bullets filled the night with a pillar of fire—

Lived by the sea,
And he frolicked in the autumn mist
In a land of Hona Lee.

Good soldiers all, the squad hadn't shot at the communist one. It had gone quietly by, the silver starlight above it, behind it, the score had been nothing to nothing, the Army the Reds. Demirgian got up: the bullet was in his chamber like a disappointed suitor, the hand grenades were on his cartridge belt, mud in the crack of their cotter pins, corrosion, dew. *But damn, I'd have fired,* he told himself while he walked to the company camp by VC all lying everywhere, kicking them— *damn, I'd have thrown a grenade, anyhow!* At times, Demirgian had walked by the Coke stand waiting until— waiting until—*I gotcha,* he had felt someone's hand at his pants pocket and he had given the Vietnamese the kicking that he deserved, he now kicked the VC bodies and he shouted at their unlistening ears, "Wake up, you silly bastard, you sorry bastard, you stupid bastard! Wake up!"

"Hey, Demirgian," a GI said, laughing. "They're already dead."

"Wake up, you goddam bastard!"

"Hey, Demirgian," the Negro radio operator said. "Don't do it."

"What do you mean don't do it?"

"Don't do it," the Negro said. He disliked brutality: once, he had been where a Negro had squatted down on a white boy, raised up a concrete block and—*down,* the boy's face had come apart like a bag of blood. And running, everyone running, the Negro radio operator running, a fruit wagon toppling over, the grapes rolling after him like bloodshot eyeballs, running, falling, when he reached home he had prayed all night, "Oh, Lord! Don't let him die!" Since then, the GI had been against brutality: still, he thought, is it brutality if they couldn't feel, if they're already dead, if their bodies lie as though fallen from sky, Demirgian kicking, calling them dirty bastards, mud of his boots spattering on the yellow faces, skin of the faces shivering like mud under raindrops— the Negro just walking off as Demirgian kicked and Demirgian cried, "Wake up! Wake up!" But none of the communist soldiers woke up.

One of the communist soldiers woke up! He looked at Demirgian with one yellow eye, an eye like a twist of lemon rind, an oily eye! He lifted one of his bloody arms! A living breathing communist, a Vietnamese of about eighteen, a Vietnamese boy, Demirgian brought down his foot on his face and—*crunch,* he felt his little nose go like a macaroon, he then asked him, "Bastard—well, was it worth it," kicking him in his eyeballs. "Stupid bastard —what did it get you," kicking him on his adam's apple. "Goddam bastard—"

THE SECRET OF VAROUJAN DEMIRGIAN. *Demirgian wants to kill commies because they are Vietnamese, that's it. A year here, Demirgian thought, and I just stand around with a finger up. And whose fault is it? Theirs— the Vietnamese people's. A cow, a tree, a rock on the railroad tracks—the people are in my goddam way, I hate them! Dead or alive—crippled, I could be blind, a basket case and they wouldn't help me! Faces the color of prunes, teeth the color of coffee grounds, mouths just like a Disposall—the breath of a garbage bag, I bet, I expect to see ants crawling out! A million, two million, I wish I were told to kill eighteen million! And then we would win the war.*

"Dumb bastard. Stupid bastard. Goddam bastard. You thought you were better than us Americans, didn't you? Ignorant bastard," Demirgian said, and he kicked at that black bag of bones until it gave consummation to Demirgian's tour and a high success to Demirgian's quest by quietly becoming dead. Congratulations, Demirgian's foot! For it hadn't been by those bullets that he had done himself proud, he had killed by his foot force alone—the bullets themselves, we ought to have saved the money, the bullets were ten cents apiece. "Sorry about that," Demirgian said to the lifeless body, and he re-entered camp by the dawn's early light, a Russian watch in his pocket, a souvenir.

Like a great headache going, a pressure on the ears relieved, the dark withdrew from Demirgian's camp, the tents became green, not gray, the brass of the bullets lay on the earth like bright little buttercups. A soldier went to police up VC, another was at the washbasin brushing his teeth, spitting the pink water into the Vietnamese mud, a toe slowly stirring the pink and the brown, washing himself, drying himself, his olive-colored towel wet with the dew, another had GI coffee from a gray aluminum cup, a taste of aluminum oxide with it, a nail in a carpenter's mouth. It was morning again, and the GIs said, "Ninety-nine days—" "Ninety-eight days—" the fewer their days the greater their hate for the Vietnamese people. No soap: there was no redeeming them, the GIs believed. *We should smear them— We should send up some tidal waves— We should put a few eggs in*—a few hard-boiled eggs having hydrogen yolks, the GIs believed. Having started like Kurtz they finished like Kurtz, *Exterminate them.*

The sun rose. At the Coke stand, it was business as usual, the Vietnamese with their betel-black teeth, the raggedy tan piaster notes, the sticky yellow paint on the soda bottles so GIs wouldn't take the empties away, the price of four times the wholesale price, the heat, the Vietnamese children saying give me—give me—and saying dirty words if they didn't get given, a woman shouting, a man shouting, *"Ong da ban chet—"* the Army had wounded his buffalo, he wanted damages. "Well," Demirgian said, "I killed me a gook," and Demirgian smiled satisfiedly, Demirgian's soul was at peace, Demirgian, a few weeks later, flew to the land in whose interests he had been posted to Asia, to that golden gate, to that WELCOME sign in red, white, and blue. A man among men, he had come marching home again. Let's give him a hearty welcome then. Hurrah.

2 /

He had come home on Pan Am to the music of *Muzak, to the violins with red woolen strings, the choco-*
late waltzes, the lemon merengues. His home front in Cali-
fornia wasn't quite as Demirgian had pictured it. The
scare stories that he had heard of hippie guerrillas in air-
port eaves, eyes at their sniperscopes, soldiers shot, and
some marines hanged, for God's sake—old wives' tales
every one, and the nervous nellies who locked themselves
in the pink OCCUPIED OCUPADO *rooms of Demirgian's plane*
to change to their civvies were all—overcautious, call it.
Paranoid, the GIs who didn't dare fly to America until
they had Colts in their shoulder holsters or hand grenades
in their "awol" bags. All quiet in California: the plane
came in, the passengers left, the sergeants said to Demir-
gian and Demirgian's friends fall in, dress right, take a
few giant steps, surname, first name, middle initial, sign
on the line, thanks, go to Fort Benning, Georgia. Assas-
sinated, the Vietnam veterans weren't: one more wonder-
ful rumor laid low.

But they weren't instant civilians, either, the thrill of
being called mister wouldn't be theirs until their two or
three years of service were up. Instead, the GIs now lived
in Georgia in a barracks with a big black stencil, like on
a lottery ticket, to tell everyone that it's one of 4,838

similar ones. Red metal cans for cigarette butts gave it a dab of color outside, the walls themselves being the color of curdled milk, of old curling and cracking piano keys, of 1941 papers in family attics—call it the brown barracks. Indoors, the color was cinder-track gray. A bare light bulb that a GI turned on awakened them all at five every day: the eggs would be before six, the flag would be before seven, and by seven they'd be asleep again in an Army truck. Or rather, the white soldiers slept, their arms on their knees, head on their arms, skull on their crossbones: death, while the Negroes would carry on, chortle, crow, the Negroes would dive for the oyster, dive, be alive, disappear, do somersaults, fly, become melted butter, and be a barrel of monkeys, really. The night before, the Negroes had usually been at a club where the singer would sing, "I want all the young ladies: put you' hands on you' hips! And say, Hell yeah! And say, HELL YEAH!" The night together: that's what the Negroes would laugh about.

"I didn't touch Diane, Jim."

"You didn't touch her physically."

"I got a heart, motherfucker."

"Sure. It just ain't got no feelin's."

"Zzzzz," the white soldiers would say. Or would listen in: Amos and Andy entertainment.

Day would break. At their destination, the GIs would dress in VC clothes: in black-colored quans and in cone-shaped hats to carry out a mission of squatting in a "VC" village as a company of officer candidates attacked them. "I wanna be a Viet'amese," the guys getting from the

*dust-ridden trucks would say. At first, it may seem curious
of Demirgian's friends to want to exhibit themselves in
the outward appearances of men they detested so. Consider, there was a GI who started hating the Vietnamese
at his very first dinner there at a restaurant known as
"Frenchie's" because of its chef's ethnic origin. Stepping
in one night for an egg-omelet sandwich, french fries,
and a beer, he had heard himself say, "An egg-omelet
sandwich," for really the umpteenth time, he had practically shouted it, the girl, though, had stared at him
through lusterless and insensible slits. She's stupid, the
GI had thought. She's ignorant, three—four—five hundred thousand soldiers here, and no real effort to understand us. She's lax, he had thought: all right, then, so
why would he want to wear quans today and to lower
himself to a Vietnamese's level? The answer, perhaps,
was exactly that: he had to lower himself, and by the
subtle evidence of his condescension he could remind
himself, and everyone else, of his superior status as an
American. Cadillacs, suits, the conquest of infantile paraly-
sis, plumbing indoors—we Americans walk on the stars
themselves.*

*"Say," a GI would say as he put some clean pants on,
"I ain't never seen no Viet'amese with starch in their
clothes."*

*"I seen some Viet'amese pretty stiff," a second soldier
allowed. "But that warn't starch!"*

*The clothes on, everyone squatted down in the "VC"
village. Orders were, as soon as they saw the whites of*

their eyes the GIs had to pretend to die to help those officer candidates prepare for Asia. "Exaggerate it! Now really ham it up," the orders were, and on cool mornings the GIs did die imaginatively: their arms in a Y-shape of agony, tongues out, eyeballs aflame, trying to expire like the $112 stunt men in The Green Berets. But hot Georgia afternoons tired them, the boys tipped their Vietnamese coolie caps and laid themselves down as lazily as Huckleberry Finns. "Cool it," they sighed as OCS fired blanks at their ears from a meter away, "Cool it, I'm already dead." At dinnertime, they sat in the truck in a silence of sour cream's consistency as they bounced back to their brown barracks.

It lasted months. And then, the Malibus the color of bluebirds and GTOs the color of lemon lollipops took the GIs from the place that the paint manufacturer's agency might say is camembert-colored out to America proper. "I'm out! O-u-not-single-t-but-triple-t-outtt," the GIs said happily. In Boston, Demirgian became a draftsman of automobile switches, and he even helped with the heater switch for the Lincoln Continental. His sergeant still was in Leavenworth, his lieutenant became a captain here in Georgia, his generals became the directors of America's big corporations. His medal writer, the Rutgers alumnus with the relentless-efforts words, went to Manhattan as the associate producer of Whirlpool commercials, "Just one of the many major innovations introduced by Whirlpool." In peace, almost everyone integrated himself with the System.

Nor were the GIs racists about it. They couldn't help it if Ford, etcetera, couldn't make use of Negroes who behaved like a barrel of Barbary apes saying, "Hell yeah. HELL YEAH." All such savage customs, the Negroes had better suppress or submit to being square pegs—to being like Vietnamese—indefinitely, in industry these only got in everything's way. A wrench: that's what the Negroes would be, and good samaritans like the Whirlpool producer tried as they formerly tried with the Vietnamese to help these impossible people fit in. Washee washee—on Mondays and Wednesdays, the Rutgers alumnus stayed after hours, he stayed there amid the Moviolas to lay equal opportunity on Negroes by showing them how to write, to shoot, to print, and to edit television commercials and to make themselves part of Madison avenue. "Now your sentence here—"

"Who took the 'which' out?"

"I did," the Rutgers alumnus said.

"What's wrong with the which?"

"It is incorrect grammatically."

"The Red Cross which helps people—"

"I was an English major, and I know which's incorrect."

"I think it's a word which's needed."

An impasse. It seemed to the good producer that the Red Cross helps people—period, it's a redundancy if a person says, "I who like candy," instead of, "I like candy," curtsy, sit down immediately. He just wasn't like the Negroes, who heard the moon, meows of black cats, *and broomsticks—something, though, in their witch's word, and who wouldn't in any good grace surrender it. Would Shakespeare? "I can play lots of games with which—"*

"I didn't write this for English professors—"

"If which isn't right, I want that—"

"I don't like the white people's language," a Negro with an Afro said. A veteran, he had been taught to use screwdrivers, certain sizes of crescent wrenches, and—it may seem temerarious—hammers, hard hammers, to repair the atomic bombs that the Demirgians thought were a final solution for Vietnam but, as a rule, were broken, a top military secret that the Negro couldn't get a shoe repairman's salary with in civilian life and he got into advertising, instead. "The white people's language, I never know how a person feel."

"I'm not laying rules," the Rutgers alumnus protested.

"The white people, they so—homogenized."

"Dig it, I'm not making you a white man." His words, conscientious words, had the Rutgers alumnus in Dutch again. He had come close to court-martial once in Vietnam, he had this infatuation for an HQ-and-HQ-company password and he had gone around in the moonlight shouting it, "Exceptional edibles!" As for which, he thought that if TV audiences from the Rio up had adjusted their ears to English aesthetics—if two hundred million people agreed, the Negroes should too. He didn't want to make these black people whiter. In spite of his

soap that was—FAST, or floated, or was soap of beautiful women, or of Hollywood stars, he didn't behave like in Aesop and he didn't try to irrationally wash the "Negro" off anyone here. The whiches and whuffos only.

"I agree with him," a Negro said suddenly. "The which rubs."

"Why does it?" The broken-bomb man.

"The which is incorrect grammatically. Dig, if I call in a secretary and say, 'Fetch me a pencil,' grammatically that's fine but if I say, 'Go get me a pencil,' then no. That's incorrect grammatically."

"Redundant," another put in.

"Redundant."

"It just depend on who you're talking to. I'm being ethnic with—"

"If you're being ethnic, talk in Swahili."

"Aw—"

"I like it better without which," a Negro girl. "It's clear. It's clean. There's no double-talk. It's clear-clut." She corrected herself, "Cut."

"I'm against the which."

In time, the Moviolas sitting by, bloated big bullfrogs —in time, the Negroes all came around to the whichless way. "I think that's heavy," a producer there with the Rutgers alumnus assured them. "You wrote a real sophisti- cated commercial. If you left in a soap-kind-of-suds-selling ending or a 125th-street delivery, well—" he didn't say it, you might be a mailroom boy interminably, to really fit *in you must rub off the ragged edges. It being eleven, the Negroes all wrapped it, rode their aluminum elevator down, and exited by a revolving door.* DON'T WALK, *the traffic light said now.* WALK, *the traffic light said now, and they walked up Madison avenue totally with it. A lesson to those recalcitrant people, the Vietnamese.*

3 / BOB

One fine morning, a Negro with an Afro as thick as this: *oooooooooooooooooooooo*, was walking by Rockefeller center cool and collectedly though he was already ten minutes late for work. Impeccably shined shoes and a glen-plaid suit let America know that he wasn't an "I gotta get a signature" messenger but an executive, a Negro in his twenties making $10,000 plus, or perhaps double plus, who could say, *I've made it, I'm an American now, I belong*. Above all, a vest of that imperceptible plaid advertised that it had happened: that the golden doors had opened wide to this great-great-grandson of Virginia slaves. *I have a dream*—no longer was it a dream for Robert Melvin.

He carried a tan attaché case. Though twelve minutes late now, Melvin had no anxieties while he walked past the diamond rings in Manhattan's windows, A FABULOUS BUY—$5,000, the five-percent signs in its savings banks, BEST BUY IN TOWN. Yet he walked fast: he looked at a $100 watch on his inside wrist and he cut through a bank to cut twenty seconds from his carefree way. *Carefree*—the Muzak machine in the elevator was playing this as Melvin stepped on. He wasn't impatient, though not until twenty-eight hundred pounds of tardy executives stood there did the elevator rise: at Melvin's floor the doors stayed open two seconds and he left leisurely—late to work by twenty minutes or twenty-five by his boss's impetuous watch. He smiled into his white boss's office. "You won't believe this," Melvin said. "I woke up this morning and I smelled smoke. My wife said, 'It must be your feet—'"

It had been smoke, though—truly, for Melvin wasn't on time because his white wooden house in the suburbs of Newark had accidentally caught fire, a $150 disaster to a Sears electric laundry drier. Melvin had had his breakfast today with ten or a dozen firemen sitting in. "I might as well forget about the seven-twelve," the commuter bus, "I'll get the seven-fifty-seven," he had said levelheadedly as the firemen drew his carbon-colored wardrobe from the Sears and shouted things like, "Tony, give me a pair of pliers!" The later commuter bus—it would get to Manhattan after nine, but Melvin had sat drinking milk in his kitchen, reaching for a kitchen knife, working the Esquire shoe polish open, and polishing with a firm spiral turn of a finger, like a man writing tiny *o*'s in a sales ledger, till the firemen left. He had then smoked a Kent while he carefully wrote,

6:45 a.m.
breakfast
just had a fire

on some stationery: then he had folded it, wrapped it around the Kents, and circled it with rubber bands, a ritual that he had held to since learning about it on TV,

How to Stop Smoking. Then he had caught the second-best bus to Manhattan as his wife whispered, "Baby," to their daughter. "Now we'll get a new drier—"

"Hey! How about that," Melvin's young boss was laughing now.

His anecdote over, Melvin went to a girl in a white nurse's uniform, got a Lily plastic cup of coffee from her, and carried it to his cubicle while the secretaries said, "Good morning, Bob," in a very flirtatious way, as though they and Melvin had some secret together, a wild dionysian night in a Xerox closet, perhaps. He hung up his glen-plaid jacket and he seated himself in his leather swivel chair—*tut* to being thirty minutes late, he had been thirty minutes early all April. An hour sometimes.

He took a pad of yellow paper from a desk drawer. Even now in his shirt sleeves—a Negro in shirt sleeves, he fitted in America's executive suites like a Bigelow rug or a Parker set on a black marble slab. Melvin really had the Image. Forget that he was athletically built, that he was six-foot-four—the thing of things was Melvin's cool, he had broken in his emotions, just a relaxed smile or a nod of his head could say, *I'm on top of things, trust me.* Furrows, fits of hysteria, tics, gnawings of nails—no, Melvin's demeanor said he could take a responsibility and he wouldn't sway. He wasn't like—no names, please, an indecisive executive here who in a few weeks would be fired, surely, for saying at conference tables, "Um— Da dum dum dum— I don't know," while chewing his Venus pencil eraser or drawing so many rococo serifs onto the word BUDGET that it soon belonged over the gateway to Versailles—his legs crossed, the sickle-shaped hair on his shins showing over his bobby socks. No, in the name of Dale Carnegie, if Melvin had to admit that he didn't *know,* he said spiritedly, "I'll find out," he didn't chew his Venuses or chewing gum, either, and as for bobby socks—*really, hasn't anyone told him?* Eight months here, and he had learned that a little line on a minus symbol makes it a plus. He had remarked once, "The three thousand dollars is not sufficient—" and he had checked himself. "Is insufficient. I'll have to use the right word," an *is* is more positive, isn't it? A few more weeks and he hoped for—he relied on—a very important promotion, such as no Negro in his company ever had had.

He had been raised near the Newark ghetto. "Robert," his parents had told him, his father an AT&T night watchman, his mother on the assembly line for Desitin ointment, "Robert, you'll be a white-collar worker someday," he took economics at Fordham and it had happened. A respectable job in Manhattan—at his pivotal cubicle the telephones sang, the Xerox purred like a happy cat, a secretary thumbed through her *Glamour,* and Melvin now pulled his sharpest pencil from his glass pencil cup. It was springtime: end of the fiscal year, and Melvin's task was to ascertain just how many million dollars he had spent in it. Difficult! for a whole $50,000 had faded, strayed, or been stolen, somehow, or had eluded the adding machines of the good-looking girls in Accounting. And so Melvin's morning began—with a coffee, a Kent, a notation,

9:50 a.m.
working
fine

meaning feeling fine, and a pleasant sense of anticipation as his dark brown fingers curled over his Venus pencil to write on his yellow scratch pad, *Scope.*

Once in the morning does it. *The scene is a wedding reception—the wedding guests get a Scope and a penciled note, Once in the morning does it, signed, the green phantom. The wedding guests say, "I do not have bad breath!" "Well, don't look at me, either!" "It can't be for me! I'm from the bride's side . . ."*

Melvin was far into advertising now, he was senior assistant account executive for a Caribbean-colored mouthwash. Scope was a brand that a man could be proud of: Scope tasted good and it tasted, somehow, *green,* it tasted ten degrees cooler than the bottle felt, in a Michelin it would be stars beyond its Micrin, Colgate, Lavoris, and Listerine competitors. The hint of Micrin's mint was so tenuous that it might almost be Scope-and-soda, and Colgate's peppermint-spearmint was so redolent of Colgate toothpaste that to gargle with it was rather unnerving. To sip of Lavoris's zinc chloride was to plant cactus on the

epithelium, try as its agency did to extol it—*pucker power*
—try as its brewers did to hide it with alcohol, cinnamon,
cloves, the spice that the mandarins sucked as they ad-
dressed emperors of the Earlier Han Dynasty. Listerine—
well, as Melvin's account executive boss put it, "Listerine's
like the inside of a motorman's glove." Nor was a jigger
of Listerine even *curiously* awful like one of Greece's ret-
sina wine, it was just—period, awful. It was enough that
the taste of Scope beat the others cold—it still worked as
well as Listerine, though, in helping us do as Ovid advised us, *Nec male odorati sit tristis anhelitus oris,* Do not
let the breath of the mouth smell bad.

A respectable item. It added each day to America's
sum total happiness at least insofar as its customers weren't
on Listerine. Still, it wasn't humanitarianism that got Melvin to his office at eight-thirty almost every day or now
pushed his Venus pencil on, a proud peacock's quill. In
fact, if Melvin had the account for Kents, the company
cigarette, instead, he would probably shout, "What a beautiful time for a Kent," before he could scribble *fine* on his
scorecard for *How to Stop Smoking.* Call it America's
paradox that his joys were all irrespective of—were really
in *spite* of the many virtues of Scope. Consider, Listerine
came in a wrapping paper of olive drab, like an Army
cannon shell, and it tasted worse. To work in its agency
was a challenge, accordingly—to have to lead people to
thymol, eucalyptol, etcetera, boric acid, to a kickapoo
brew and to make people drink it. *"But it's so strong,"* "So
is bad breath," when a Listerine ad was effective its execu-

tives felt the same sense of accomplishment that lay in doing the *Times*'s diagramless crossword puzzle or in winning in Vietnam, somehow. It was an Annapurna, Listerine! And uptown at Scope the opposite held—the executives had a few qualms that if eighteen million people used Scope it wasn't due to their efforts, only to tasty domiphen bromide.

No, Melvin was someone normal. At nine every day, he reached into his inbox—if nine hours later he had raised everything into his outbox, he felt with pride that he had performed a foot-pound of indispensable work. A half world from Asia, he was content to have fitted himself into the green machine of Scope—a little wheel in the wheelworks, sure, a dumb second lieutenant here but a unit without which the System would stop. In other words, to get eighteen million people down to a drugstore with a dollar-and-something each was a job well beyond the competence of Melvin or anyone else. It required a thousand associates, each an exquisite expert in a thousandth part of the enterprise, each a man very anxious to Do His Bit. Each indispensable, and Melvin was one. It wasn't in doing good in this world that he prided himself, it was in doing—period, in getting a $50,000 question and *answering* it, a $50,000,000 sales goal and *meeting* it, a—

Well. It was to woo away those dogged users of Listerine, etcetera, that the "creatives" at Melvin's company thought up the green phantom, a fictional character who at wedding receptions, on Navy destroyers, in schoolrooms, on Vespas of city meter maids, and at other colorful *mise en scènes* secretly left a Scope bottle with the scribbled note, "Once in the morning does it." People in California who had watched the phantom's antics since 1967 had switched to Scope in such numbers that all of the mouthwash's hopes rode on the phantom now—he would go national soon, he would fill up a pause in a CBS beauty contest and do his thing daily after that. Do not suppose, though, that the wedding-reception commercial could be just threaded up, press the green button, *go*—everyone out in CBS land enjoy it. Far from it, Melvin would have to put that $50,000 treasure hunt off, again off, again *off*, as this or that sudden emergency gave the green phantom pause. In fact, he had just written the *Scope* on his yellow pad, he had just written under it,

jas   ond   jfm   amj

the months of the fiscal year and such numbers as 406.4 and 441.7 thousands of dollars, when the real thrills of America began. A secretary put *Glamour* down to deliver three of her pink "someone telephoned" slips to the tardy assistant executive—all three arose from a Jewish producer of a diametrically opposite temperament. Where the Negro might say, "It is urgent to call me," the Jewish producer's messages said, "Call me or I'll scream." And so Melvin dialed—and it was soon *sorry about that* to those fifty G's as Melvin, his glen-plaid jacket back on, was sliding down in the elevator while the Muzak played *Chloe* with bated breath. *"Taxi,"* he said on Fifth avenue. His fellow worker, the Jewish producer, meanwhile, saying, "I'll be at— Darling, I'll be at— *Darling*," stamping then at a daydreaming secretary, "I'll be at MPO," hurtled down in the elevator, and he threw himself into Melvin's taxi as though he had cossacks after him. A film editor also dove in.

They had reason to. The wedding reception dated to 1967, remember. It had struck—it had just thunderstruck everyone that the passing years had made mischief with the wedding reception's final line of "Get new Scope! Once in the morning does it," Scope was no longer *new* now. It needed another final line, and so Melvin sat in a taxi today because affairs sent him to MPO—to MPO studios—to listen to a new announcer say, "Get Scope! Once in the morning does it." Melvin would have a studio from one to one-thirty, but it was such a jam-packed day it was already twelve-forty-five. As sanguine as Melvin seemed, if CBS didn't have his Scope commercial soon he would owe it a $250 lateness fee—he would have to pay $57,150 instead of just $56,900, the normal cost of interrupting a CBS beauty contest for a sixtieth part of an hour. "Step on it, driver," the Jewish producer in his horse-blanket jacket cried. Alas, no less sense of urgency rode in ten thousand other cars, the Scope and Cope and Scott and Cott—the businessmen of Manhattan sat staring at twelve-forty-fives saying, "Step on it, driver," the taxis responded, stole into the intersections, crossed the T and stopped there, the traffic lights went red—green—the taxis, though, had stuck themselves into a Chinese puzzle that all of the mayor's horses couldn't undo, not a tire tread moved. The taxis climbed on each other's fenders—all courtesy fled, the taxis passed soot on each other or they signaled dirty words with OFF DUTY signs. Gas and oil turned to carbon monoxide, electricity to ear-shattering sounds, as the drivers sent up burnt offerings and eighty-decibel prayers to the gods of velocity to get these anxious executives to MPO and Manhattan's other cathedrals of commerce. *Honk!*

South of Melvin's horseless carriage, the "Once in the morning" announcer had saved his pennies and stolen time by just slipping like an Indian in between the belligerent bumpers. At the studio, he had waited—waited—while a Crest commercial for the CBS beauty contest sang, "I'm not exactly the ugliest girl! I've got good hair. Good skin—" (*Oh goodness,* the announcer thought, *that is so heartless! To tell those girls if they've got a mole, they're losers*)—he had waited there in a Ralston checkerboard shirt and a knitted wool tie as the ominous hands of a wall clock rolled past one-ten.

And then, the door burst open and Scope people flew in, Melvin okay after running a ten-minute mile. No one exchanged any "How do you do"s, the Jewish producer hadn't time and he thrust the announcer a Xerox of his imminent task. It came in a fresh manila envelope, though it could fit in a fortune cookie:

Before the green phantom strikes you . . . get Scope!
Once in the morning does it.

The announcer read it and practically gasped, "This is it?" After thirty years in communications, he was still overwhelmed that two to three thousand dollars would be his for just saying seventeen syllables—*oh goodness,* for $3.92 he could cable them all to Zanzibar via satellite. Already, he had $1,000 today for talking like the World's Meanest Man, *My greatest caper was buyin' up every roll of Kodak film. And right before a beautiful summer weekend—*

"This has to be done in four-and-a-half seconds," the producer said.

"Oh boy. Four-and-a-half," the announcer replied. "The last line. Should it be *Once in the morning does it,* or *Once in the morning does it.*" His voice had an I-am-a-little-birdie quality in his first rendition that in his second one he resisted.

"In between," the producer said.

"Closer to the second one," Melvin corrected him.

"In between. Closer to the second," the producer said.

"Once in the morning does it," the announcer said.

"That's it," Melvin said.

"I like it better your way, Bob," the film editor agreed.

Melvin felt a small ball of warmth inside him at this challenge given and challenge met. Remember, *Once in the morning does it* wasn't doggerel but a wizard's words that had turned domiphen bromide and cetylpyridium chloride into America's number-two mouthwash and had sent competitors fleeing to *Webster's* for synonyms for dawn-to-dawn security, the Listerine agency doing its thing, *It's strong! It's got to be strong to last long,* and Lavoris trying,

> *The pucker lasts for minutes*
> *But the cleaning power in it*
> *Lasts for hour after hour—*
> *Pucker power!*

Melvin's choice was no trivial one, thousands of dollars rode on every inflection of *Once in the morning does it,* Melvin knew it, Melvin loved it, Melvin worked in the kitchen where the heat was. He was no lonely "corporation nigger" with an office by the reception room but a slot on the organizational chart at the terminus of a dotted line, he was no *quote* coordinator of equal opportunities or a manager of special markets—of Negro markets, thank you no. He had further duties than to eat chicken croquettes at the Urban Coalition Dinner. "Closer to the second one," a million billion electrons would dance in transistors to Melvin's tune, and soon every infinitesimal dot of America's ether would go exactly—*so,* from the redwood forests to the White House.

"I feel like Darryl Zanuck," Melvin said, and he sat down in a black leather director's chair. "Roll it!"

"Stand by," a studio engineer cried, then he hit a switch and a roll of tape started turning. "Take one!"

"Before the green phantom strikes you, get Scope. Once," the announcer said, he had his knitted tie loose, he was vigorous with his index finger, he gestured though there were no cameras for it, "Once in the morning does it."

"Okay," the producer said. "Try to be more confident, though."

"Stand by," the engineer said. "Take two!"

". . . Once in the morning does it."

"Try to be more intimate," the producer said.

"Stand by," the engineer said. "Take three!"

". . . Once in the morning does it."

"Too strong," the producer said. "Keep the confidential tone."

"Stand by," the engineer said. "Take four!"

". . . Once in the morning does it."

"Go faster," the producer said. "It's got to be in four seconds. Four point two."

"Stand by," the engineer said. "Take five!"

Melvin had taken his stopwatch out to twiddle with it. The wall clock was at one-twenty—in ten more minutes they'd pull the plug, the studio would be a pumpkin and Melvin a $250 loser. Until now, Melvin had never sat in a leather director's chair—oh, in Newark, at garden parties, but he had never supervised in TV till now, it could make him or break him. He was up—well, he supposed he was up for promotion to full account executive for Zest, an aquamarine toilet soap. On the elevator a few days earlier, the Muzak had taken a short intermission and he had ended the unearthly silence by asking the Zest executive, an Englishman, "What's new?" "Haven't you heard?"

"No, I haven't." "I'm quitting." *"You're shitting,"* Melvin had gasped, for he guessed that now he could make it: could be the first executive there who was Negro, too. *I'm sorry, Bill— I'm sorry, Bill— I'm sorry, Ernie*—no men of Melvin's race had gone beyond senior assistant at Melvin's company. It had, in fact, sooner or later, fired them all, a coincidence that to Melvin might mean it was being fair and square with its Negro employees, it didn't want any Negro window dummies. Didn't even the ads in Negro magazines say, WE'LL GIVE YOU THE CHANCE TO BE FIRED,

> *You'll have the chance to find out if you've got what it takes to move up. If you don't . . .*

The hopeful assistant executive had Indian ears now, to ensure that the sales pitch wouldn't seem to be "Gets Cope!"

"Stand by," the engineer said. "Take fourteen!"

". . . Once in the morning does it."

"Umm."

The producer rocked back in his swivel chair. He had heard people say a TV commercial must be an opera, a ballet, a Broadway play. A few nights ago, on Broadway, he hadn't let a nuance elude him at Nicol Williamson's *Hamlet.* He had heard civility turn to irony as Hamlet put a half second's sibilance onto the second syllable of his salutation to Rosencrantz and Guildenstern, "My *ex—*cellent good friends." Nor had he missed the cool rebuke to Claudius in Hamlet's reply, "I shall in all my best obey— *you,* madam," and he had heard resolution blow hot and cold in the course of one fast pentameter, "Now might I do it pat— *Now he is praying,*" foiled again. He thought that no less professionalism should lurk in "Once in the morning does it," *Hamlet,* on Broadway, would have to run until 2026 to be heard by as many people as CBS's new beauty contest.

"Do it again," the producer said.

"Stand by," the engineer said. "Take fifteen!"

". . . Once in the morning does it," the announcer said.

"That's good," the producer exclaimed—well, he could wish for a bit less temerity in the *does it* but this was a minor matter, *it was minuscule,* he was telling himself, he was satisfied. "Bob, are you satisfied?"

"Yes yes! Bravo," Melvin replied.

"Nice working with you, Bob," the announcer said.

"Thank you, thank you," Melvin replied. It was twenty-eight after one. Success.

The next day, he was at work at his usual eight-forty-five. His left index finger hit his Burroughs adding machine with a firm tap tap, his thumb bumped the plus-key in his renewed search for the $50,000 that had vanished with the snows of the past fiscal year. In his right hand, his Venus put tidy numbers onto his yellow pad. Yellow light with no shadows filled his cubicle like Jello or like those miraculous glows that the Byzantines saw in their navels sometimes—it was as though yellow light were an attribute of America's air. *Ummmmm,* the ubiquitous hum of those yellow tubes let Melvin be seemingly in a bee-loud glade. A buzz—a faraway telephone, a few little footfalls later, till by ten the sounds were as susurrant as a morning mass, the secretaries were at parallel desks with a *Cosmo* or a paperback—

"How is it, Ann?"

"It's all about egos and superegos. It's scary."

"Do you mean scary or— Bob? Are we disturbing you?"

"What?"

"Are we disturbing you by talking?"

Melvin smiled at the secretary over the cubicle wall. "Not too much," he teased her, really he hadn't heard her. Melvin gave every cell of himself to his working day, at eight-forty-five his cerebrum, his arm muscles, his left and right risorius, his hammer, anvil, and stirrup of his middle ears, his heart, in fact—his body and soul hired itself out to Scope or just softly dissolved. As he spoke, his left index finger went to his adding machine like God's on the Sistine ceiling—it did work while his four other fingers stayed utterly limp. His talent today and tomorrow was to stay undefiled by the unessential—by *Cosmo*s, by Sufi poetry, yoyos, soprano recorders, yoga, or reveries of just going rowing in Central park. He screwed himself into the System as tight as the adding machine's little gears or the turbines whose two hundred thousand volts fed TV transmission towers, or as Westinghouse selectomatic elevators, Muzak, GE fluorescent light bulbs, Bell telephones,

Burroughs— He tore something from the adding machine.

Eureka—or rather, a fifth of it. Melvin had just found a $10,000 error, a redhead down in Accounting (*A lovable girl. But sometimes,* Melvin thought now)—a redhead whose job it had been to add $5,000 had subtracted it, Melvin was now just $40,000 shy. He crushed the adding-machine paper into a ball, dropped it into his steel wastepaper basket—into the plastic coffee cup in the basket, too (he had played basketball for Fordham once) as his left hand picked up his telephone before it had rung twice. "Bob Melvin," Melvin said.

"Robert!" The voice on the telephone drew so many useless curlicues on Melvin's first name, it had to belong to—

"Orlando. Where were you?" Melvin said. Orlando was a Negro down in Accounting in whose lightheaded entries the $40,000 might lurk—or so Melvin had been hoping.

"Oh Robert—"

"Afraid you would melt in the rain today?" It was pouring out.

"Oh Robert! Do you know someone swiped my car top? Swiped my convertible car top! So now I've an all-year-round convertible, and I can't come in out of the—"

"We want a day's work out of you."

"But Robert! How can I do a day's work if I get here at ten-fifteen?"

"Orlando, I'll be there in—" Melvin looked at his watch irrelevantly—"I'll be a couple of minutes."

"Ciao, Robert," Orlando said.

Melvin hung up. "I'm going down to Orlando's. You know how long it normally—*takes,"* he announced, the *takes* rising way up the musical scale like the parting remarks of a passenger in a Paris-bound balloon.

In fact, there could be nothing short or sweet to Orlando's job. Orlando and nine assistants had to sit with union agreements thicker than the tables of trigonometric functions to calculate what the actors, actresses, announcers, in TV commercials were due—it was an Einstein's work. For instance: if CBS ran the wedding reception every week, the "Once in the morning" announcer stood to get $2,712 every year. But this would be $360 if CBS only ran it in Kalamazoo and $148 petty cash if the announcer *sang* it in Kalamazoo with a barbershop quartet. Still, as Melvin stood in the elevator with its *Sioux City Sue! I'm gonna rope and tie her up, I'll use my old lasso*—as Melvin tapped, he reflected that he would be prisoner not of Orlando's double entries but of Orlando himself. Orlando fitted into the Scope machine like a wooden shoe—a barefooted foot, he had even danced the *bouchade* with an African troupe prior to his business career. Orlando would be—*Orlando,* if Melvin didn't use human relations to try to remodel him. *Hiya, brother,* if Melvin was friendly he would be still sitting there on Saturday hearing about the rain, convertible cars, canvas, tents, and Ringling Brothers Barnum & Bailey. *Orlando! Come to the point, please,* if Melvin was businesslike with him he would get no place fast, it was like throwing blows at a Japanese judo champion or like thrusting from the first position at Scaramouche. No other way: Melvin had to be friendly though firm.

He left the elevator at Orlando's floor. The lovable girls in Accounting looked up from their travel brochures, *Un hôtel de style,* to welcome him as though he carried a mandolin instead of a yellow scratch pad, "Helloooo, Bob," Orlando's old secretary shut up a volume out of her grandmother's attic, *Mr. Leigh, I cannot accept the ring. Why not, Miss Edna,* Orlando was on a telephone saying, "Oh, we can—*party*," and making misnomers out of the words white-collar-worker by wearing a see-through shirt of Italian blue and a yellow apache neckerchief instead of a Polo tie. "Robert," he said as Melvin frowned in a firm though friendly way, "Robert, what time is it?"

"Twelve-twenty," Melvin said—he had twisted his watch to his outside wrist, to where he could watch it.

"Twelve-*twen*-ty," Orlando repeated, just to suck honeysuckle from the syllable *twen*. "I'll call after lunchtime—*ciao*," he said on the telephone, then he hung up and pirouetted to Melvin in his swivel chair. "I call you Robert. But you can call me anything as long as it's nice."

"Well, that's an impossibility," Melvin kidded him.

"I wonder who's calling me," Orlando continued, and he turned to his telephone again. "Oh hi, Katherine! Oh no—"

Melvin smiled weakly. He didn't light up a Kent, even though he had answered *often or always* to test question ten on *How to Stop Smoking: I light up a cigarette when*

I feel upset. Lest his choler rise to the upper tolerances of being friendly though firm, he arrested it with little appreciative chuckles. He laughed to Orlando's secretary, "Terrible, isn't he," while his fingers under the desk did a nervous flute solo on his pencil there. When he had logged enough time as Orlando's friend, he snapped his fingers, saying, "Get rid of this person!"

"I'll get back to you, Katherine," Orlando was saying —was hanging up. "Now, Robert. Hand me those readouts, would you? I'm tired."

"I know," Melvin kidded him. "It happens when you sleep too long," and he passed him perhaps ten pounds of IBM rosters of TV actors and earnings. "Can we do this in fifteen minutes, Orlando?"

"Robert! I don't know what we *have* to do in fifteen minutes."

"Yes, you do," Melvin said, and he cited a Scope commercial where there was a miscalculation, perhaps.

Orlando went through the IBMs elaborately. "We had *ichi ni san shi*—we had four people on camera," he calculated in Japanese. "And one more."

"Four plus one is five," Melvin said.

"And we had twenty and twenty-four *u*-ses," Orlando now kissed the *u* and continued.

"That is—"

"Now hang on, Robert. We've got to do this le-*git*-i-mate-ly," and he swiveled to take his arithmetic to his adding machine. Though he didn't totally close his eyes, his fingers were Wanda Landowska's.

Melvin scraped his thumbnail over his pencil-eraser sleeve. *He is the most inefficient guy,* Melvin thought, Orlando couldn't add or flip through the IBMs or just press a telephone button if he didn't embezzle ten extra seconds to savor its sensory pleasures, he couldn't even say, "Legitimately," until he had tasted every last *t* as though it had cherry liqueur inside. The five senses—rinse them in Rinso, Melvin believed, be attached to the twentieth century and in Rome do as Romans do.

"*Oh*—" Orlando said as his adding machine reported to him that twenty and twenty-four are forty-four. "What am I putting this on the machine for, I'm not very *adapt* today."

"When in Rome, Orlando—"

"Well, we're in Rome now," Orlando promised. "I'm not roamin' around now, I'm stabilized. I'm going to give you dollars only, Bob."

"All right," Melvin said.

"I'm not going to give you cents."

"Round them off."

"It's so much easier without cents."

"Pun intended?"

"Robert! That was a no-no," Orlando said, Orlando was as impatient today as Melvin was. The senior assistant executive was a saddity in Orlando's book—*a square, a real country boy,* Orlando thought, a Negro so soulless that on Saturdays he mowed the grass, perhaps, or he shopped for a salt-and-pepper set for Mother's day—he then had it wrapped in pink paper and a pink satin ribbon

63

that the saleslady tied in a double bow. In fact, Melvin had done approximately that on Saturday last—the pink satin bow, though, was a prefab, the saleslady at a Newark suburban department store had pressed the side inscribed PRESS TO PACKAGE to Melvin's package, a Mother's day notary seal, and Melvin had looked from his *objet d'art* to his wristwatch thinking, *I didn't do badly,* door to door in just forty-five minutes. A salt shaker, a pepper mill, a lawn mower, a lawn—*so what,* it didn't seem to Orlando that the senior assistant for Scope jars had profited much in this world by his losing soul. His heart still beat, his blood circulated, his body didn't swing from a sour-apple tree, but if everything that was Negro in him beyond the first millimeter and if everything that was Melvin in him ceased at eight-forty-five—well, was it or wasn't it death? "In dollars," Orlando continued, "the *money*-terry value is two thousand and seventy. And five percent for pension and welfare."

"I'll have to disagree with you," Melvin replied.

"Okay. We had five people on camera—oh, Robert," Orlando said. "My stomach is growling so!"

"Oh lord have mercy," Orlando's secretary laughed.

"Yes," Melvin agreed with her.

"The lord has just answered us," Orlando said, and he stood up and carried his stomach off to the company cafeteria.

Melvin ate at Toots's alone. An extra dry Tanqueray martini with an olive settled him, he had pot roast and he

went to Orlando's again in midafternoon. He found a
$290 infirmity in Orlando's arithmetic—that's all, though
an hour later he found the $40,000 upstairs, $40,000 and
plenty more!

WHERE THE $40,000 WAS, OR CHERCHEZ LA FEMME.
*"I'm just thrilled with it!" "I'm glad you're happy, dar-
ling." "It's the loveliest coat! And the nicest present! And
the sweetest thing!" "I'm glad, darling." "Tune in again
tomorrow for The Edge of Night!"*
And for a Scope commercial, doubtlessly. Was it because there are seven days to a week? seven stars to a dip-
per? whatever, one of those lovable girls in Accounting
had multiplied seven times all of *Edge*'s entries. Her total
was seven times what it should be—"Bob," a time buyer,
upstairs, telling him, "I see a significant error of $90,000."
A treasure chest, and Melvin now celebrated the Fordham
way. He picked up a crumpled paper from the time
buyer's floor—it was really the *Gunsmoke* summer rerun
list, he bent his knees and he tossed it towards a toy basketball basket on the time buyer's wall. It went swish—a
solid two points for Melvin, he was an AP honorable
mention once.

He took his elevator up. This morning, Melvin was
someone with a $50,000 shortage—add in $10,000 and
$90,000 and it was without abracadabra a $50,000 surplus.
And yet—an IBM readout wasn't a wallet, an error's an

error and it didn't make a dime's worth of difference cler-
ically. As was clear to Melvin, a day of right turns had
returned him to virtually where he had started from at
eight-forty-five. He felt really emasculated today. He felt
trapped like an ant inside of his inbox, circling clockwise,
using his God-given hours in this endless search for an
exit light. To his *left*—right—*left*—right—he could still
be in Vietnam itself. "I've got— After all that bullshit," he
told another account man on the elevator, "I've got
$50,000 now."

"I've got one that beats that all—"

"To hell," Melvin guessed as the doors clipped the
sentence off. He walked to his windowless cubicle—well,
it had a paper-poster window of Fifth avenue's cars. He
put down his yellow scratch pad, he suddenly—*hopped,* he
tapped the celotex ceiling, he whispered, "Two points,"
he brushed the celotex dust from his fingertips. Years ago,
he had hoped to play professionally with the Knicks—
now he was twenty-seven, still he had hopes to release
himself from a system that was at times, *at times,* that of a
rat in a rattrap, perhaps. The senior assistant executive had
a Plan. It wasn't to become a Knick any longer, a hippie,
an African dancer, a kid with the Morning Star Commune
in California. It wasn't to simply drop out—it was to become the account man for Zest and the boss of someone
whose duty was to play mickey mouse every day. A see-
through window, a secretary, a senior assistant slave all
his own! Ninety-nine bottles, ninety-eight bottles—or as

the rock lyrics said it, *Any day now, any day now, I shall be released.*

Good news, Melvin would go to Hollywood soon on company business—to Hollywood! A year ago, he had sold gasoline, oil, automobile tires for a Manhattan firm, it wouldn't even send him to Rochester till it had asked everyone, "Do you mind if our sales representative's colored?" In his blue clothes, he had explained sanitation to gas-station managers by washing the ladies' and gentlemen's rooms, a plumber's rubber suction cup in his grasp —now he would fly to Hollywood with an attaché case. Up and away!

His trip to the city of lights! camera! action! owed to the actress whose line at the wedding reception was "I can assure you one and all. I do not have bad breath." *Bad breath*—that was an Americanism, the TV commissioners in Canada drew a firm ball-point line at *runny noses,* at *pimples,* at *blackheads,* at all imputations of anyone's *bad breath.* To satisfy them, the actress had done another three feet of film saying—no, everyone, not *"Je n'ai pas haleine forte,"* but "I do not have a breath problem," an elegance that the Canadians wouldn't stamp a NOT APPROVED on and, incidentally, would earn the actress another $120 of Orlando's money. Call it kismet, though, the three feet of film weren't in Hollywood now—were missing now. So swore a lady executive in a Bonwit's suit.

"Oh boy boy boy," Melvin had told her. "I have a problem."

"I think we can rectify it. Somehow."

"I love it," Melvin had suddenly told her—Melvin had meant it. Now, Melvin would have to dub that wedding-reception commercial in a Hollywood dubbing studio. Stand by, America! To think—out of every dollar for Scope a fraction would go into kerosene to permit a pilot to fly an executive to watch a producer to direct an actress to say in Hollywood, California, "I do not have a breath problem," what a remarkable world this is! The fuel would use up thirty-five tons of oxygen, as much as two hundred thousand people—as much as the Newark ghetto would. Our atmosphere would be forty-eight tons of carbon dioxide richer, the earth would be warmer, the icebergs smaller, the Atlantic higher—the hour would be closer when all of Manhattan's cubicles would be awash in salt water and Melvin's wet yellow pad adrift over the Statue of Liberty's head.

Meanwhile—Melvin sat at his adding machine the unwilling heir to $50,000. At times, he moaned in a mock-exasperated way, "The budget!" When his stomach called, he ate corned beef and cabbage from a polystyrene mess-kit with a polystyrene cover, the company cafeteria special. Or, despite rain, he ate hot dogs at Nathan's while the other assistant executives talked ethics, "I don't want to sell something if I know it causes lung disease." "What? You wouldn't try to put your brand in the best possible light?" "But if it—" "Bob. If they asked you to be the account executive for—" "*Of course,*" then to the adding machine again. He kept on California-dreaming until one day the sun rolled down on Manhattan like a basket full of fresh oranges: a beautiful day. Eighty degrees, the secretaries went to a birthday party at the Italian Pavilion, and Melvin said yes to his boss's invitation to eat shrimp and Brittany crepes at an outdoors restaurant in Central park.

In it the hippies did dances in Baghdad beads, and the kids from the Krishna society sang, "Krishna Krishna! Hare hare," as their finger cymbals tinkled like the silver things of a Himalayan caravan. Tan awnings softened the sunlight on Ford models, college girls in see-through sweaters, actresses, black cats in Muhammad hats, hedonists, fashion photographers in Fu mustaches, gallerygoers, gourmets, and Melvin in this glorious place. "I'll have a Tanqueray martini—" thank you no, Melvin passed up the ad establishment's *ordinaire* today, he had sangria though he kept to advertising talk, to California, lovable girls at adding machines, actors, once in the morning does it, competitive copy. "Lavoris came up with something new," he said to his young white boss. "The pucker lasts for minutes but the pucker power in it—*hour after hour.*"

"Once in the morning does it," his boss observed.

"Do you know about that one, Tom? The announcer said did we want it *Once in the morning does it* or *Once in the morning does it.* Howard," the Jewish producer, "said in between but closer to the first one. I said the second one."

His boss nodded pleasantly, and he ordered the Brittany crepes—after the coffee the Scope executives left. The silver-bell trees, the daffodils there, the living things seemed to open themselves to let sunshine out. An orange balloon flew on Burns's statue—Burns's thumb and his forefinger held it, another balloon soared off to Oz as children cried, "Look at it go!" Hippies came up from the bear cages saying beautiful things, "And the underwear was in all different colors!" *"Oh no,"* a chick with the hippies laughed. A camel looked at Scope's people curiously, and a few flirty schoolgirls identified them by Melvin's gray vest.

"Hello businessmen!"

"Hello," Melvin answered them.

The white teenyboppers blushed. Truly, there was no corner to Melvin's world where a Negro was someone apart. The racism—it was just something he read about in the newspapers, almost. He had even heard white boys in Newark ask, "Is he your daddy?" "No, is he yours?" Even the firemen—the white firemen in their undershirts had even lifted up Melvin's baby, "Are you all right, little girl," and the white men on Melvin's commuter buses sat by him unashamedly. His company had a Negro in one of every twelve jobs, and it didn't ask any, "Are you for riots?" "Are you for Stokely Carmichael?" "Are you for H. Rap Brown?" It didn't tell a Negro executive, "We would send you to Hollywood but if the actress—" "But if the studio engineer—" *"But if."* Fellow workers of Melvin's asked him to paper basketball games, his boss bought him Brittany crepes, the girls flirted till it was scandalous, "Bob? How much is nine times six?" "Fifty-four." "Really?" "Really! It's been fifty-four for years now." "*Giggle*." On the elevators, his friends kidded him as they kidded any Caucasian, "First floor, please," and Melvin answered, "I want to make doorman next."

Yes, he had that rarest right of a Negro, to make a mistake or two without the company thinking, *well, we tried*. It seemed clear to Melvin, though, that a cubicle with a paper window might just be a fool's paradise—that a Negro assistant might have his Afro tight up against its celotex ceiling. After all, no Negro at Melvin's company had ever climbed a second step, "He just has no—presence," executives said. Just a few weeks ago, a Negro organization had advertised in the *Times,*

Congratulations! Your company is making progress. You've just handed a $10,000 a year job to another black man. Another black man has made it—to the bottom.

So it didn't seem a test of Melvin's competence but of America's when he set head, heart, soul on getting out of the bottoms and on becoming the Zest man. No better time to advance his ambitions than now—a halcyon day, as Melvin and Melvin's boss strolled in Central park. He did it most matter-of-factly.

"What's with the Zest account, Tom?" Melvin asked.

"He is leaving us," his boss replied uninformatively—

he meant the English executive. "Going to go to Switzerland."

"*Switzerland,*" Melvin whistled. "That is a change in
the *shed*-yool."

His boss laughed at Melvin's impersonation.

"Well, Tom, I hope I'm being considered for—" *No,*
Melvin was a cool enough cat to say nothing more. Let the
mills of the gods grind slowly.

What a glorious day! A golden calliope ground out
East Side, West Side. In the street there was sunshine in
seven colors—it had to be waded through, people who
started across when the light was at WALK didn't get to the
sidewalk till it was solid DONT WALK. The sky was Italian
blue everywhere—except where the letters THE G passed
across it, the unfinished text of a skywriter pilot that the
forty floors of Melvin's skyscraper hid. "Maybe it'll be THE
GREEN PHANTOM," his boss kidded—kidded, since if anyone
in Manhattan knew how Scope wasn't into skywriting in
this fiscal year, it was he ("We don't know if people look
at it," the space buyers said). So it was curious that the next
fleecy cloud to go over was R. The next one—as Melvin's
spellbound boss said, "Gee, it's an E."

It just was anything-can-happen day. Coming towards
them, a sexy young blonde turned to look at the letters
too. "Oh wow, what is it," she asked them, her French
sailing shoes north, her head twisted south, her hand on
a copy of *Blood, Sweat & Tears.* "Are you in business?"

"Why?"

"I'm going to throw pebbles—stones—*rocks*—at type-writers. I don't want to be a career girl," the girl said to Melvin's boss.

"How about a nun?"

"I don't want all that garbage."

"Do you act?"

"*Yes,*" the girl laughed, as the giant letters THE GREE drifted over her. "I was at two auditions today and— Oh, this is crazy. I don't sing so I played the kazoo." And pulling one out, she serenaded the Scope executives with *My Country 'Tis of Thee.* The woolly letters THE GREEN rode by.

"I hope the next letter isn't P. I really do," Melvin's boss said.

"Zzz zzz *zzz* zzz zzz," the kazooist concluded. "Is it THE GREEN GIANT?"

It wasn't—the skywriter flew a quarter mile to skip a space, and he blew everyone the letter s. "The green some-thing," Melvin's boss reported, he whipped his sunglasses off, he strode to the elevator, and he went through the Westinghouse electric eye, Melvin beside him. But the lazy elevator doors took a tenth of a second extra to start to close, for on warm spring, summer, and Indian-summer days the resistance rose in the relay potentiometers on the twenty-fourth floor.

Upstairs, the secretaries ate a vanilla birthday cake and set fire to a cylinder made of the onionskin wrapper of a Lazzaroni macaroon, the *dolce* at the Italian Pavilion. The air in the onionskin rose and—"*Oh, fabulous,*" the secretaries cried as the onionskin soared away, a fiery moth. The birthday girl had a yoyo and—

> *A birthday gift from all of us,*
> *And loads of wishes, too,*
> *For all the best of everything,*
> *In days ahead of you.*

"You won't believe it," Melvin's boss informed his secretary. "We were walking down Fifth avenue—"

"And you saw Troy Donahue."

"We looked up. And it's not a bird, it's not a plane, it's skywriting. And it's spelling G—R—"

"E—E—" his secretary guessed.

"But as this transpired the letter s came across."

"So what was it," his secretary asked.

"Oh, I didn't have half an hour to—"

Melvin went to his cubicle telling himself, *A three-hour lunch. I bet I've got twenty telephone calls,* it was practically so. A sheaf of pink telephone slips lay on his blotter, and Melvin now began dialing them. "Boy oh boy," he said kiddingly, "the client has a lot of nerve calling me. Making me look through my inbox and—oh, John, hello," he said to a Scope executive in Toronto who asked him, is *I do not have a breath problem* ready? "Asap. As soon as possible. Nice talking with you, John. Hello, John," he said to a Scope man in Cincinnati who asked him, en route to Hollywood could he see unobtrusively how Scope was doing in Kansas City? "It would be easy. Goodbye, John. Hello, Howard. *Oh no*," Melvin cried, and he hurried down to the Jewish producer whispering, "And then there were none."

A few minutes later, he sat in a screening room as the wedding-reception commercial went on. *"I can assure you,"* the actress began in a close-up. *"I do not have bad breath."*

"See, Bob," the Jewish producer whispered. "When she lifts her tongue you can see the *th*."

"Bad *breath-th*," Melvin muttered. "And we want *breath-th* problem."

"Can't we say something like, I do not have poor breath," the producer whispered.

"We can't," Melvin said.

"I don't know what to tell you, Bob. Okay," the producer told him. "If we dub it, it's going to look dubbed."

Arrivederci Hollywood, Melvin had tripped on a tongue tip on his way towards the Wild West. "I'm letting the steam off," Melvin said while softly slapping the stainless steel of his elevator car. A lesser executive might roar or writhe on a Bigelow—

> *When in trouble, when in doubt,*
> *Run in circles, scream and shout,*

as the saying goes, but a public show of emotion wasn't for Melvin if it didn't contribute to Scope. He was cool as a custard—*controlled,* as he told his boss, "If we dub it, it's going to look woefully out of sync, I'm afraid," if they filmed it fresh for Canada it would be $25,000, unthinkable.

"We'll have to bite the bullet," his boss replied.

Melvin walked back to his cubicle—to his warm telephone, he called his Canadian client back, he broke the news gently: no new commercials for Canada. "I recommend, John," he said while his Venus did doodles over a lawn-mower ad in the Newark *Star-Ledger,* "I recommend, in the absence of additional sixties, that we keep current sixties on air in Canada until we can implement our media plan," and Melvin walked back to his boss's office. "I just spoke to John," Melvin said.

"John decided to quit," his boss kidded him.

"I sold him. At least I think I have," Melvin said, and he walked back to his cubicle. He put down his yellow scratch pad—it stirred the air, it sent telephone slips to the floor, he picked them up. He then began dialing again. "Hello, Frank," he said to a Scope man who advised him of a new accounting error, he was $90,000 in debt again. "Thank you, Frank. Hello, Vaughan," he said to a Negro who asked him about a football player with the Buffalo Bills. "He doesn't go to his right side, dig it? Goodbye, Vaughan. Hello, Howard. *What?*" Melvin gasped. *"He located it?"* Earth overturn, for Melvin had learned that a film of a Hollywood actress saying, "I do not have a breath problem," had just been found in Secaucus—in *Secaucus*—in a warehouse across from the Lumberland lumberyards. It had been in a can labeled WEPPING till a man in Secaucus guessed that the word might be scribbledygook for a wedding reception. And so Melvin walked to his boss's office again. "Are you ready for this? They've got the Canadian film."

"Incompetence!"

It was something new—Melvin's boss shouted this. His face became red, an emotion, rare as the mumps, discolored it and misshaped it. His body stiffened—*enough is enough,* the boss thought, he thought that if every employee there were to die, decease, somehow drown in the water coolers, it seriously would be a godsend to Scope's new wedding-reception commercial. It had been built, after all, of immaculate facts, immobile, immutable, and as immune as a pot of plastic ivy to man's idiosyncrasies. It wasn't built of subjective stuff.

X people watch television.
Y people watch CBS contests.
Z people have halitosis—

total, if they and their demographics were fed to an IBM machine, in a split millisecond the IBM readout would tell you, I CAN ASSURE YOU ONE AND ALL. I DO NOT HAVE, etcetera, the whole wedding-reception commercial. It would practically film it, a process that a man, mouse, temperamental bat—a living thing in the circuitry couldn't help. It only could hinder, such as by writing WEPPING on this wedding commercial with no apprehension that it may become brown in Secaucus like a lost little worm or a Dead Sea Scroll. The endemic incalculability of Man was what was intolerable to Melvin's boss. A man either cured it or Melvin's boss found himself hating him, a *curse* on Hollywood actresses, on Accounting girls, on Melvin sometimes, on Jewish producers—

"I'll kill him if I can get him."

And saying so, Melvin's boss started after the Jewish producer. He didn't bring an Army rifle, he had been talking rhetorically, apparently, he wasn't quite like the sweet-smiling sergeant but if a look could kill—the producer had had it. Providentially, when the killer came the Jewish producer was already out—already at MPO with the Ralston red-shirt announcer taking him through the finale of Canada's wedding reception, *Funny how the people at table fourteen didn't know they needed Scope. But the green phantom did!*

"Give it a more intimate quality."

". . . But the green phantom did!"

"Give it a slier quality."

". . . But the green phantom did!"

"It's a grotesquerie now."

". . . But the green phantom did!"

"Be like the shadow knows."

". . . But the green shadow did. *Ha*," the announcer apologized.

Melvin went to his cubicle—to his paper window and to his cardboard CHICKEN LITTLE WAS RIGHT sign. He hoped that his boss's outburst was at that careless producer only —at Howard. He telephoned his Canadian client again, "Hello, John." He thought, *I want a cigarette and I can't have it for forty-eight—for thirty hours,* a couple days of cold turkey were the latest on *How to Stop Smoking.* He remembered today was Friday as a secretary with her fingers over her mouth in embarrassment said, "I forgot all *about* you, Bob. I went to get your paycheck and—" He went to the subway station at ten past six. "It's terrible," he heard someone in the station say. "Now this is the third straight F," there wasn't an E until twenty past. He looked at the subway posters saying to spend his $10,000 plus on Israel bonds, Anacin aspirins, Kent cigarettes, L&M cigarettes, Miller's beer, and *The Green Slime,* a Japanese movie. He missed the six-twenty-five, he took the seven suburban train, he wasn't home until after eight. His pretty wife sat in the kitchen as she braided the baby's hair. "How did it go at the office, darling—" *never,* she never asked that, her husband's world used a language only the Babylonians understood, the films of a Canadian commercial were the *elements of a Canadian execution— love* was a Scope commercial whose final line was "I love you." And so Melvin's wife simply kissed him, "Hi," and his daughter, aged two, reached her hand out.

*"Gimme fi'," *the baby cried.

And he understood it. Melvin smiled wide as they shared in a soul brothers' handshake—give me five fingers, slap! From the radio there came a soul-station sound: an Aretha song, and Melvin now danced the tighten up to it. *You treated me mean, you treated me cruel! Chain chain chain, chain o' fools,* the family that can tighten up can lighten up, the father, mother, baby all danced it, the baby doing the toddle up—

"You got it, baby, shake it!"

"Yeah," Melvin said.

OR AS RALPH WALDO EMERSON SAID, *"The gentleman is the complement of whatever person [he] converses with. He will outpray saints in chapel, outgeneral veterans in the field, and outshine all courtesy in the hall. He is good company for pirates and academicians . . ."*

Melvin was a high-school freshman when the essay on *Manners* met his eye. *"He is good company . . ."* he had copied this, he carried it inside his wallet with his business cards, his four credit cards, his Playboy club membership cards—it never left him. It meant to Melvin that to proceed down his spinal cord and to configure himself in Scope mode by turning a thousand switches off—on Mondays this was appropriate, but on weekends it was gentlemanly to put himself on personality two. It was good manners if Melvin did as Negroes did by divesting his Wallach's suit and sunning himself in glad rags on Saturdays and Sundays. Unlike the 1860 to 1960 black bourgeoisie who'd as soon be seen in tribal scars as wearing an Afro, or talking in Zulu as telling you, "Dig it, Jim—" unlike these, the Melvin generation saw no shame in these foofaraws from the family attic. Say it loud, he was *proud* that he not only danced the fox trot but the tighten up and that blindfolded he could tell the collard greens from the Brussels sprouts. A few hours' acclimation time, and he could become a perfect round peg in a Negro neighborhood. So it was without anxiety that on Saturday night, the lawn being cut, he appeared at a Newark gymnasium in red satin shorts and a shirt with a red number fifteen to play basketball with a few other one-time greats from the Newark ghetto. Melvin, as it were, tuned himself to a soul-music station—come in, Orange High.

"Hiya, Slim. Hiya, Slats," Melvin said to the other players, and he slapped their hands like a man dealing twenty-one. "I haven't seen you in a long while, baby." He knew, of course, as happy as these people were on a basketball court with a clean yellow smell of Valspar, the truth is they earned as little as $7,500 and he alone had a job a daughter might say of, "My father is—" A mainte-nance man, a machinist out at American Can—

> *He never learned a trade, he just sells gas,*
> *Checks oil, and changes flats. Once in a while*
> *As a gag he dribbles an inner tube.*

The bitter truth is, Melvin alone had a job that wasn't in Newark's ghetto and in the same social class as the tire dribbler's of Updike's *Ex-Basketball Player.* Man to man against him there was a Seagram's salesman, a Goliath given to telling him, "Liquor is the biggest business there is. There is nothing as—*big,* as liquor," the salesman one of the five great basketball players of history, an AP All-Time All-American.

Melvin played center. For one whose muscles rested on cotton felt on Monday, Tuesday, Wednesday, Thurs-day, and Friday, he played well, he could still hold a basketball as serenely as Yorick's skull till the very tenth of a second that he—*cut loose,* when he leapt at the basket he could still hang as gracefully as Plisetskaya till the Seagram's salesman crashed back to earth like a shot rhinoceros, then he would ever so lightly—*shoot.* But he would miss, and though he had once turned the Fordham students into Apaches by sinking four in the last three minutes, now it was many minutes before he had even scored once. The other players teased him, "How about that? One for twenty."

"One for four. Watch it, daddy," Melvin said, but he wasn't proud of it. For weeks now, he hadn't held a basketball heavier than a quarter ounce. He knew, unless a muscle is used every day it unravels like an old celery stalk, even the lawn mower gave him a charley horse in his shoulder today, he couldn't follow through with his lay-ups—*boy,* he kept telling himself, *this is my worst winter ever.* His side having lost, he went to the shower room, and he said to the liquor salesman in Madison-avenue language, "Whew! That is a wrap!"

"I ain' goin' out there again," the salesman said.

"I ain' goin' out there either. I have had—" Melvin said in Negro talk, and he just sighed, he didn't say *it.* "I fucked with the lawn all day," he continued, stretching his elbows behind him as a stork sometimes does, to loosen his charley horse. "I'm goin' to sleep tonight, boy."

"You ain' goin' get a taste with us?"

"Well—I will if Momma let me," Melvin said.

Momma did. An hour later, he showed up inside a bar

where the basketball players splashed in a Seagram's bottle and shouted, twisted apart the pistachio nuts, let gravity choose where the nutshells went, put their elbows—*where?* had no Woolworth napkins but caught life in their little circle as though it were *it*. Melvin himself was no stranger at Robby's bar, Melvin since he was eighteen had eaten potato chips and tasted ale at Newark's many ghetto bars. "Hey, let it all hang out," he said, and he walked inside. He clapped his hands to Aretha to exhibit that he was good company among the Ballantine signs and soul songs here—as good as behind the white tablecloths of Toots's, in Tanqueray dry-martini land. "Hey, brother. Give me a Ballantine's ale," he said to a daydreamer here in a bartender's apron—the bartender didn't hear it.

"Hey, brother," a man with a Kent attempted. "If the bartender able to tender this bar, I say *please*—a Ballantine's ale!" No reaction—the bartender was as pottery-eared as a bottle of orange curaçao. A silence ensued.

"That's the company cigarette," Melvin told the Kent smoker.

"What—?"

"That's the company cigarette."

"Oh—? Hey you quit smokin', Bob?"

"What—?"

"Hey you quit smokin'?"

"What am I smoking?"

"Hey! Did you quit smoking yet, Bob?"

"Oh, I been tryin' to," Melvin said. "See, I been watchin' this TV show, *How to Stop Smokin'*. And the cat says to wrap up you' cigarette pack in a piece o' paper, a rubber band, and—"

"Hey, mister bar-*ten*-der! You standin' there with you' hands in you' pocket, lover boy, a Ballantine's ale!"

The startled bartender looked their way—he poured it. Melvin took his pilsner glass to a table where there was so much chatter about a Fordham and NYU game of six seasons past, it practically blew the foam off Melvin's ale.

"Bob was on *you*," a basketball player from NYU said.

"Bob wasn't on me, Neil was on me," Melvin said. "No, I guess Bob was."

"Bob was on you until it got crucial."

"Yeah—" Melvin remembered.

"Barry was on you until he got taken out."

"Yeah—! I enjoyed playin' him," Melvin remembered. "I knew he had heart because he—*cried,* when he got taken out. I mean he *cried,* man," it came easier now. The sentences came to Melvin's lips, and they swished through without his measuring every word as though he were shooting it from forty feet out. "We were runnin' a pass-and-go-opposite pattern," he continued. "Know what he said to me? Barry said, 'Come on, motherfucker, drive,' " and Melvin's new dialect was just letter-perfect here, his *i* was three miles wide and it vanished past the horizon before it had ever reached the *v.* "I said, 'No, man. I got the pill.' He said, *'Motherfucker, driiiiiii—'* Silence, my song is playing," he suddenly said, and he began dancing now to *Grazin' in the Grass.* The rhythm flowed like perspiration from Melvin's sides.

"Do your thing," the others cried. "You ever see Walter dance? He left Newark he really lost it."

"I'm better than him," Melvin laughed.

"Sure you is!"

Melvin could feel the music inside him. *It's real, so real, so real, so real,* and Melvin continued the tighten up, his feet never touched the floor, his hands were (as Updike puts it)—*wild birds,* he shook off a vest of cloth or canvas or coco matting that he had worn without knowing it. Something in Melvin was kissed by the Ballantine's and it stirred like a sleeping beauty. "I gonna—*gichoo,*" he cried, and he threw a wrestler's nelson onto the Seagram's salesman. The man sent a playful elbow to Melvin's belly, "*Oo—!* Motherfucker, don't fuck with me," Melvin laughed, the salesman rolled into him in a double mattress, the room tilted like a dump truck, and Melvin, the salesman, everyone fell out of Robby's bar. They laughed as they dribbled their heads on Newark's hot concrete, tied one another to Newark's new lampposts, by Newark's mercury vapor lamps all became blue—oh, Mona, what a night that was! It was beautiful! The tobacco pipes and Kent packs and glasses, ears, elbows hid in the gutters or sidewalk cracks as the basketball players went at it— the breath rose out of Melvin's lungs, it floated away and he couldn't catch it again because of his laughing so . . .

He heard the basketball players look for a lost tobacco pipe. "It was a twelve-dollar pipe!" "Was it o' sen'imental value?" "Was ten dollar worth o' herbs in it?" Melvin could hear the hue and cry, Melvin, though, didn't join in

it, Melvin lay on the sidewalk under a NO PARKING STAND-
ING STOPPING sign, no longer breathing hard, no longer
stiff—the bruise by his right eye no longer hurting him.
His ribs receded into the concrete that he had once
roller-skated on and shouted *home free all* on. No pore in
Melvin was closed now—no longer did he route himself
like a train trying to get to Hoboken but he flowed out of
himself and into himself like the ocean's edges. He felt
alive.

"Want me to help you up, Bob?"

The blur between him and the Dippers composed itself into a Negro's face. "Yeah. Help me up," Melvin said.
And he walked back to the barroom before any Newark
police could come by and arrest the senior assistant account
man for Scope.

He was at his cubicle on Monday morning. "The
budget," he sighed, his firm piano tuner's fingers on his
adding machine, a pale yellow shirt on, a tie, a tiny brass
cornucopia clasp, his thoughts on the spoor of that $90,000
—a blackness big as a meadow mushroom under his right
eye. He had been—*splowed,* on Saturday, so utterly that
he had forgotten to write,

11:00
drinking ale
splowed

on his company stationery, his outer wrapper to Kents. Ale and his own connivance mistreated the English language that day—he remembered that, *I ain't gonna go* was illiterate, *I been trying to* should be *I've*. His old sport shirt—well, it wasn't impeccable, was it? Melvin didn't really care, Melvin recalled, *There is nothing settled in manners,* the day had Emerson's sanction. Once in Newark the supererogatory letter *r* had dropped onto Melvin's tongue tip as Melvin was saying impeccable—he said impreccable, instead, he was embarrassed so! Better to say it colloquially, *sharp as a meat axe, man,* it was better to commit solecisms and easy elisions, *a piece o' paper*—a bottle of ale, it was better than a Tanqueray when a gentleman's out in Negro company. *I know,* Melvin now told himself, *they're a little loud but I've a right to a little fun.* "Robert Melvin," Melvin said—his telephone had been ringing.

"Bob," the voice there was Melvin's boss's, "I just figured out in my little pea brain that we cannot be *cannot* be $90,000 short."

"Oh—?"

"So what do you think of that barrel of apples?"

"I'll work on it," Melvin sighed, and he punched up the 90,000 on his adding machine, a nine that curled like a flower late in September, a zero that ran in a circle to nowhere, a zero that ran—he wasn't himself today. Mud, runny soap in a soap dish, mucilage, scum—a still liquid was in Melvin's arteries today, it stuck and it didn't circulate. His malaise had no anatomical center like the Monday blues, *Monday morning. And people are starting off wrong with the Monday morning blahs,* a seltzer commercial put it—Melvin did too. "I've the Monday blahs. It doesn't get me excited, work," he told telephone callers till at a few minutes to twelve there came a telephone call so—*electric,* that the Bell system seemed to have routed it through his spinal cord, he straightened as though from a hundred volts, he rallied from the Melvin blahs.

"Bob—" he recognized the vice-president on whose red carpet all Negro assistants here had sooner or later heard, "I'm sorry," but a vice-president with the more cordial duty of choosing the next account man for Zest. "Bob, can I talk to you a minute?"

"Any time you say."

"Right now."

Now, it was plainer than day to Melvin that he could only be fired through racism of the most vicious and Mississippi sort. It had been something subtler with the Negroes before him, Negroes who really didn't fit in America's corporations. Just so much softness, firmness, openness, sureness, patience, push, an ear here, an eye there, a smile no wider than—*so,* the fitting form of Manhattan was a cast-iron one, the Negroes had never taken its measure. *Too much,* too little, *too much,* one minute the Negroes would be shy shrinking violets—be Georges in railway cars, a minute later and they couldn't say "Yessir" if forty lashes inspired them, the VP had fired them. But Melvin? His idiocratic talent was to fit

into offices even if his ofay associates didn't give him a—
slap, every second minute and do a dynamite tighten up.
The line between overacquiescence and overassertion, if
Melvin couldn't toe it nobody could, he could *belong* or
no Negro businessman could. "I'll be right down," he said,
and he hurried there with a throbbing heart. It faltered
when he saw instantly that he wouldn't be the account
man for Zest.

"Sit down, Bob, would you? I'll be a minute only,"
the VP, all sideburns, like an awesome OUR FOUNDER
portrait, said. On his drawerless desk, the VP had heap
after heap of human legs: or he seemed to, though all of
them emanated from the VP and a big white account
executive for Prell shampoo. Not far from the Prell man
lay three hexahedrons of aquamarine: three bars of Zest,
his chatter was Zest, it was there on his yellow scratch
pad, *Zest,* he was clearly the new account man for Zest.
"So you're in that canoe," the VP was telling him.

The big white executive drew on a Tueros cigar.
Melvin's left outer ankle lay on Melvin's knee, and his
socks invited the VP's eye. His pants pressed themselves
to a red leather couch—a couch on a carpet were two of
the three perquisites of the higher executives here. On the
drawerless desk—the third—was a full-color advertise-
ment for CREST ALMIGHTY that was facetious, surely, or
so Melvin felt, and a photograph: a wife so well scrubbed
that she couldn't but be a rebuff to the *black is beautiful*
theory. The big white executive and the VP continued
talking, and Melvin continued sitting there. Once in

Newark, up for class president, as the votes came in Melvin had kept becomingly cool by just thinking trigonometry, now he kept thinking of anything other than— *Do not think of it.* Outside, the Plaza hotel had a green copper roof.

His bruise hurt. "Bob," he suddenly heard the VP say. "The reason you're here is I'm asking you—no, I'm telling you. Welcome to Prell Concentrate."

To what—? To Prell—? Melvin's first job at this company was as a junior assistant for that semiliquid and Scope-colored shampoo—a junior, an adding machinist, that's all, a fingernail. In his eyes there was no anxiety, though, as Melvin asked the VP, "Is that as account executive?"

And the VP laughed. "Of *course* as account executive."

"I'm flabbergasted," Melvin said.

"I'd like it to be effective as of Monday. Catch," the VP continued, and he threw a Prell tube to Melvin. "Do you use it?"

A pause. "Yes."

"It's a fun brand. It's really—*wild,* the current campaign. Do you know about it?"

"Yes, I do," Melvin said. "Are you contemplating sixties?"

"Thirties."

"You are contemplating thirties," Melvin said, and he wrote *thirties* on his yellow pad.

"You'll have an all-girl writer group," the VP continued.

"A harem," the Tueros cigar smoker said.

"You'll have an assistant—er," and the VP paused, the VP scraped some of the protoplasm from his fingertip. The assistant for Prell shampoo was that bobby-soxer, *I— I—I don't understand.* "So you'll be saddled with George," the VP admitted.

"We're $140,000 over," the Tueros cigar smoker said.

"And we go to production of new commercials on Monday. Bob," the VP continued. "A lot of people bugged me about being considered for Prell. Sometimes things come to those who don't seek it, though, like you. So welcome to Prell Concentrate."

"Thank you," Melvin said on a rising note. He walked off, he stepped on the elevator, he went to his cubicle— it wouldn't be his cubicle, he would have a room through whose tubes of Prell the sunlight fell in a luminous pool of Caribbean color. *I can throw out my paper window now,* Melvin remembered. *What a way to chase the Monday blahs.* He leapt up, clicking his heels, and he whispered, "Whoopee."

To bob from accounting: *This is a very special, And important time for you, And so congratulations, And the best of wishes, too.*

"It's a new world now," Melvin said on the phone to his family, his friends. "I was sitting here in my office, and I was kind of Monday pissed-off—" "I had this bullshit work to do—" "I was just miserable and—" "*I was promoted, I'm an account executive now—*" "I'm dancing around—" "I'm on a cloud—" "I'm feeling high, and I haven't had—"

"So you'll get a raise," his wife interrupted him.

"Probably—"

"Not probably but for sure!"

And stock options, too—it meant a new laundry drier for Melvin's wife. It all owed to Melvin's competence that he had come up life's ladder to Prell shampoo—to his skill in whittling himself and in fitting in. Melvin the *Negro* was invisible here—he truly was, it was a paradox, though, that to Melvin his skin seemed to burn about him as fierce as a Florida suntan today. All of his other thoughts yielded to—*Prell belongs to a Negro now,* it just overpowered him, it pushed to his consciousness like the bubbles in boiling water. *Melvin,* by Horatio Alger. He couldn't forget his kindergarten now, "He called me a Niger," he rhymed it with tiger, he ran to his teacher crying one day. "Bobby," the teacher had promised him, "someday you'll be a successful man." He couldn't forget how he had been taunted in Madison Square Garden, "Shoot, black boy! Shoot!" How in Washington he had asked for Virginia Gentleman, "Where did you get the money, boy?" He couldn't forget: in Newark, the guardsmen had spread him against his Rambler, had slapped at his torso, his thighs, had found no Colt automatics, had ordered him, "No driving in Newark, mister!" And now! The world's greatest advertiser was Prell's manufacturer—was Procter & Gamble, and Melvin was its first account man who was Negro. A carpet, a couch, a desk without drawers—could they be far behind now?

"I must say it surprised me," Melvin said at the cocktail hour. "It isn't that I'm incompetent but—"

"Let us hope it will typify," a Negro proposed.

"I'll drink to it," Melvin answered.

He really didn't have to. Already, Negroes of Melvin's ability sat as high as the eightieth floor of America's corporations. Cigarette lighters and chewing gum—Negroes were the comptroller–vice-presidents of Ronson and Beech-Nut, Negroes now were vice-presidents at CBS, Burlington, Bank of America, Greyhound, Macy's, and Pepsi-Cola. At Clairol, a Negro with a MALCOLM pin of two inches' radius sat in a swivel chair of eighty percent cotton felt and twenty percent urethane foam. Negroes were the brand managers of All laundry soap, Woolite sweater soap, L&M cigarettes, Negroes in advertising were the account executives for Lux soap, Rinso laundry soap, Spry shortening, Drive laundry soap, Planter's peanuts, and Eastern airlines—for *Pan Am makes the going great* and for

> *Schaefer's*
> *Is the one beer to have*
> *When you're having more than one.*

Attaché cases of alligator, pig, lamb, lizard, calf, and African elephant—Abraham Lincoln, the Negroes now fitted in.

4 /

*So cheers. And here's to Negroes everywhere
making it. Because even as Melvin lifted his Tanqueray
glass, the Negroes of Newark lifted up Gallo bottles tonight—the Negroes rioted, and the Molotov cocktails
there were the bottled howls of "We are men too."
Pebbles, stones, rocks, the Molotovs, guns, the Negroes
were using anything to become men now. "I'll drink to it,"
Melvin said, Melvin left on the nine-twenty-five and he
rode through another riot—the Negro basketball players,
perhaps, the Negro atomic repairman beat up a Jewish
hippie chick, a Negro veteran raped the zzz-zzz kazooist,
sending her to a mental hospital in Princeton, New Jersey.*

*It was imminent: the Second Civil War, the Negroes
declared. Alerted, the Army got waterproof maps of
America and told every soldier at the brown barracks
that he might use a real bullet again, click, clack, and
he might operate in this hemisphere—somewhat, the
officers said, as his forefathers did in the wars against
the Seminoles and the Sioux. No more farces in "VC"
villages—if a riot started, it would devolve on those veterans of Asia to do their thing in America, instead. The
starch soldier, the washee-washee soldier, the egg-omelet-
sandwich soldier—if trouble came, the boys at Fort Benning, Georgia, were going in.*

And the Negroes too. "In the Army there is one color. And that's olive drab," the Army believed, though the Army's color was no longer olive drab and the Army's own post newspaper had real-estate advertisements for Colored and real-estate advertisements for Whites. At the barracks, the Negroes were people apart, the Negroes all rode together, got dressed in VC quans together, died in a VC village together—the Negroes had even agreed, "We should have a club."

"The soul brothers club."

"It should be association."

"No, social association."

"I'll be the treasurer."

"I'll be the president," a Negro whose name was Thompson had volunteered. A boy raised in Dunn, North Carolina, a cotton picker, a founder of NAACP there, a tobacco picker, when he had been drafted he had been working in Newark and printing the word NYLON *on paintbrush handles.*

"I'll be the secretary."

"I'll be the social director—"

A club there would be. As president, Thompson had gone to a neighborhood printer, he had gone temporarily awol to get some SOUL BROTHERS SOCIAL ASSOCIATION *membership cards. He was shown several logos like*

and *and* (SHELL) *and, after passing over a star saying, "It for the boy scouts," a star and a crescent saying, "It for the masons," and a bulldog saying, "It un-*

friendly," he had settled on the shaking hands and on *Cheltenham* type. At night, he had written the *Bylaws* while coincidentally watching the CBS beauty contest and even chipping in, "*She bat her eye too much*," "*She lick her lip too much*," "*I see they ain't got no soul sisters here*," "*She eat Wheaties, I think*."

"*We'll be right back after this word about the green phantom*."

"*The green phantom*," Thompson murmured.

"*Well, I can assure you one and all. I do not have bad breath*."

"*Bad breath*."

"*I tell you*," a Negro said to Thompson. "*When you eat those garlic hot dogs—*"

He had worked until five. "*For better or worse, we're friends*," his *Bylaws* began. "*On becoming a member there is a fee of ten dollar. A member will be obliged to do his part as a member—*" Ten pages long, it still wasn't clear from the *Bylaws* what the soul brothers social association would do. "*The soul brothers social association support—er*," Thompson had thought aloud at four-forty-five. "*It support the Red Cross*." In fact, though it seems inappropriate the Negroes in the brown barracks wanted what the Negro rioters wanted, "*We are men too*." A uniform notwithstanding, the Negroes all felt somewhat lesser than men—as Thompson, for instance, felt on the afternoon that he tried to join the American Legion. By just walking in, Thompson had startled everyone there. It might be some odious toad that a Legionnaire saw as *with fingers spread he sought to use sorcery to exorcise the incubus from its squatting place in the vestibule. "No, every post in America is the judge of its membership," the Legionnaire said as Thompson now almost shriveled away. "No, every post in America—"*

Typical. It was a wonder, really, that the soul society didn't put a Molotov cocktail in its canteen and go riot itself. In town, the movies weren't segregated but Negroes were barred from the roller rink on the weekends and on Mondays, Wednesdays, and Fridays—it had happened once to the association's own secretary. The owners of Coke stands sometimes said, "No, we won't serve you," it had happened once to the treasurer when he sought to buy sandwiches to sustain him at iron attention at the burial of a Vietnam casualty, a Negro himself. At night, when the soul brothers drove to Aretha clubs to listen to "Chain chain chain," the city police would wait for a few to come rolling outside to piss underneath a NO PARKING STANDING STOPPING *sign, "Now come to the station, pisser-takers." At the same time, the white soldiers went to a club where the MC would hold up underwear drawers saying that they were Martin Luther King's. "But what is the brown? It is nigger ass. A nigger, of course," the MC would add, "a nigger is ass all over."*

"Haha," the whites would say.

To the brothers, it was just racism, obviously—not so. If the white people didn't have use for the Negroes, the Negroes were themselves at fault for it. Erratic, extemporaneous, alive, the Negroes ran riot inside of our iron machinery and were disliked, disparaged—well, the Negroes were envied, actually. After all, America was nothing if not a wheelworks, a case of interconnecting cogs as critically built as a Rolex. If one small gear had a missing tooth, if one went impulsively slower, faster, another way, or went whirling away like a Frisbee, if one became lost in Secaucus, somehow—a disaster, the whole damned machine would die. To prevent it, everything, everything, had to cleanse itself of the arbitrary and to fit squarely in. Not just matériel—also men, an American who went around to music inside himself was a threat to the self-respect and the self-preservation of everyone else. An anathema—as a Negro was.

It wasn't because of racism, though. A man could be brown as the coconuts—as Melvin, and pass inspection if he suppressed whatever was in the system's way. Of course, the Negroes at the brown barracks might have a trying time of it. To push domiphen bromide down a man's throat wasn't awfully hard—a bayonet was. To bully a Negro for being as one oneself is, for saying as one oneself does, "I am a man, everyone—" it was hard, it was contrary to conscience, and it was hubris, perhaps, when the Army didn't think that its Negroes might have the aspirations of Indians, not white men. If a riot started, the Negroes would go to it—period paragraph, the Army announced, and it then announced classes on how everyone in the barracks ought to comport himself on domestic coordinates.

The teachers would be a white second lieutenant and a white sergeant. "I could start off by bullshitting, sergeant," the lieutenant suggested one day. "Something like, 'Gentlemen, we are gathered here on this auspicious occasion to instill—'" looking down at the lesson plan the Army had given them to see what he must instill. A silence: then the lieutenant murmured, "It gets pretty flowery, doesn't it?"

"If it sails over the head of Private Joe Doakes," the sergeant replied, "we ought to revise it. He won't be there carrying a dictionary."

"Right," the lieutenant said. In the lesson plan, he had spotted as many (a) and (b) and (c)s as bullet holes in a rifleman's target or ʃ-signs in Einstein. "Discuss the psychological influences . . ." Even at its simplest, even in such subsections as (1)(e)(1)(b) where the Army said fiery speakers initiate riots by waving their arms and hammering hard on their rostrums—there too, the Army overestimated Private Joe Doakes. "Note," continued the lesson plan. "Cite Hitler."

An impracticality. Hitler was dead before the GIs were babies. "No. We have to mention here," the sergeant suggested, "some of our skillful agitators is Stokely Carmichael and— Now what's the other one?"

"Stokes," the lieutenant said.

"Stokey," the sergeant said.

"Stokely," the lieutenant said.

"And Rap Brown," the sergeant remembered. He smiled—he was making the lesson plan as GI-digestible

as Gerber's. "Do you know what those riots in Newark cost? Ten million dollars, sir," the sergeant said.

"Newark's bad, I was there," the lieutenant agreed. "The population distribution favors the Negroes. If they really get going—"

"Well. We will do a new lesson plan," the sergeant said. And the stage was set.

5 / VANTEE

A few days later, the GIs of the brown barracks sat in a dark auditorium an hour after reveille call. A pall of damp atmosphere lay on each soldier's shoulders like a sopping wet poncho, and a smell of wet leather arose from the seat underneath him. No other light but a photoflood in a tin reflector was on—a thousand watts, it didn't so much illumine the speaker's stand as administer the third degree on the orchestra seats to let sergeants know who to growl at, "Hey, sleeping beauty. Wake up." In this glare, it was unscientific of the white second lieutenant to commence with a stimulus to those retinopathic eyes and to try to interest these boys in Riots by visual aids. A lot cleverer might be a *Playboy* party joke or a limerick—but no, the lieutenant said, "Gentlemen! What we want to teach you is listed here," on a wooden easel, and he lifted a piece of provocative canvas to unveil a color photograph of Michelle Hamilton of Pasadena, California, the Playmate for March. "And if," the lieutenant giggled, "if that doesn't cause a riot, I don't know what will."

No one laughed. The silence owed to the photoflood, the bulb beneath which the photograph fell on the optic nerves like an Anuskiewicz.

"Can everyone see?" Undaunted, the lieutenant took

off Michelle to show everyone an honest-to-God list of what he would teach them. It was printed in pale-green artist's ink—it was just psychedelic, man. It shimmered like a faraway cactus, though if glimpsed from the corner of either eye it fell into focus as CROWD CHARACTERISTICS and other phrases in English. "First in the lesson plan is crowd characteristics," the lieutenant said. "Sergeant!" And the white sergeant went to the rostrum.

He used the Socratic method. "Private," he said to a boy in the M or Nth row, a Negro, "what is a crowd?"

"Motherfucker. I'm getting it this morning," the GI whispered while he pulled himself up.

"What is a crowd?"

"A crowd is a bunch of people."

"What?"

"You've got to bear with me, sergeant. I got a cold," untrue. With the rest of the soul brothers social association, he had been doing boogaloos to Aretha at a night-club for Negroes until the hour of reveille minus two. "A crowd is a bunch of people gets together."

"Thank you."

"You're welcome," the soldier said. He sat down again, a flaw of Socratic method being that he fell asleep safe in the knowledge that all further cries of "Private" wouldn't mean him.

The boys called it "Harassment." A month of instruction in characteristics of crowds, of clowns, of Christ knows who—it was just harassment, the strategy of their officers to get an Army of dumb driven cattle, all dully amenable to every imbecile order. "I tell you, I'm cracking like a mother," the president of the soul association whispered now—Thompson whispered now. "I got to tell myself that if cat is c-a-t and if dog is d-o-g, I'm not cracking yet." As that sergeant twaddled on, Thompson sat in a pilgrim's posture on the twenty-fourth hour in the pillory. He watched as his wristwatch melted like a warm pat of butter on rye, he waited to write in his spiral notebook something besides,

> *Some come here to sit and think,*
> *Some come here to wonder—*

a quatrain that he had seen on the auditorium's lavatory wall. He tried, at times, to recollect what the Constitution says about crowds just to pester the sergeant with it, *Congress shall make no law abridging*—and he whispered to a Negro nearby, "What is that amen'ment?" He told a few jokes, furthermore, unaware that in a month's time (to the hour, almost)—in a month's time, he would be ordered into a city of one million people with his riot rifle, his bayonet, his gray grenades of CS tear gas pinned on like boutonnieres, an infantryman in America.

"Gentlemen," the sergeant asked them. "How do we identify in a crowd, its leader?"

"Take me to you' leader," the president whispered.

Out out, damned drowsiness, out. An overdose of downers and an antidote of uppers were the Rx, customarily—it was dexedrine time, the sergeant knew. "Gentlemen? Time for a joke," he announced, and then he began it. "There was this little girl, all right? And this little girl . . ."

Stop me if you've heard this, ". . . *was tugging at her mother's skirt, asking, "Mommy, can I have a baby?" "Of course not, dear," the mother replied, without missing a stroke in her ironing. "Are you sure?" the little girl persisted. "Certainly," said the mother. As she ran to rejoin her playmates in the yard, the child called out, "OK, fellas! Same game!"*

Copyright 1966 by Playboy magazine. All through the sexy sixties, the sergeant had gotten his *Playboys* in his monthly mail out of a higher desire than to peep at one:three representations of girly-girls. It was close, though: he had subscribed to get those anthologies of *Playboy*'s party jokes on the overleaf of the playmate page. *"Then there was the sleepy bride who couldn't stay awake for a second." "Then there was . . ."* Though he hadn't scissored these out of *Playboy* and alphabetized them in a filing box of A tabs for androgynes and B tabs for brides, with a Bic he had written the *Playboy* jokes on some three-by-fives and he had filed these, yes, in a filing box, to use as other teachers use *Bartlett's* whenever he had to communicate with GIs at seven o'clock. Like the Polynesian nymphomaniac who always longed for Samoa, *Copyright 1967,* the conscientious sergeant went far beyond the call of his duties. He knew that if riots started, the GIs would be America's last precious hope—if their bayonets failed, the Bastille would fall. "Do you know," he intended to say today, "what the riots in Newark cost us? Ten million dollars! Enough," he would say, "for a GI to go get himself a real good prostitute." The sergeant thought that he ought to use anything short of goosing them to keep these students awake.

His catalog of *Playboy* jokes, the sergeant had at his bachelor quarters in Georgia. "My wife and I, lieutenant," he once confessed with a look of I-am-a-man I-can-take-it, "after sixteen years, we found that we didn't get along." Alas, in the packing process the three-by-fives full of *"Then there was"*s may have drifted into the lady's custody. Yesterday, the sergeant had emptied the cartons and cartons of Kiwi, needles and OD threads, OD underwear, Brasso, celluloid to keep collars down, OD boot bands, buckles, alarms set at six o'clock. No luck and no card catalog: and he had slept on the sober thought that he must recite the *Playboy* jokes from his memory, which didn't contain the punch line of *"OK, fellas! Same game!"*

"Okay, fellas. I told you," concluded the sergeant. "You don't have a thing to worry about."

From the GIs, a purr as soft as a tummy rumble rose at *Playboy*'s disabled joke. A few in that drowsy auditorium said, "Ha." Encouraged by this clinical sign of life, the sergeant started to wave his arms overhead and to hammer impassionedly on his rostrum to answer his question of one minute earlier, how to identify the leaders of crowds—this was a class in Riots, remember.

"We got our— Private, wake up," the sergeant began.

"Sergeant, I is woke up!"

"We got our U.S. agitators like Stokely Carmichael and Brother—" the sergeant went on. He then turned to the lieutenant, unable to pry from his tongue tip the Rag or Rat name of that other agitator.

"Brother Rap."

"Rap Brown," the sergeant remembered.

Well! It was as though a transom had been soundlessly opened. As though the old condensation on the sagging cement floor had suddenly—*rippled,* there was a delicate stir, a silence, really, when the Negroes heard that the sergeant's old indefinable crowd was, if undressed of its euphemism—was simply the race of Americans whose leaders were Stokely and Rap. It was nothing but Negroes with baseball bats, Negroes with hunting guns, Negroes with Molotov cocktails—niggers, that's what a crowd was. As quietly as when fuses go, Thompson's eyelids rose and the pupils appeared. The president once was a Stokely or Rap himself, "Look in the colored section! What do you always see? *Swange,*" he had shouted in Dunn, North Carolina, as he thrust a hand at his audience full of gestural filth. "So tell me, how many people want to be treated as women and men whereas the Constitution promises us? How many people are for N-double-ACP? *Stand up,*" the audience in the tenement rising like GIs

at *On your feet*. Today, though, it wasn't in Thompson's
nature to pounce up in whitey's own auditorium. "Got to
act plain and simple," his grandfather often told him.
"Got to let white people think, that if they think you're
dumb and ignorant that is the truth." Down in Dunn
seeking work on cotton or cucumber farms, Thompson
would say, "I ain' got a job 'n' I sho' is needin' one,"
while he bore himself as dilapidatedly as a coat on a coat-
rack or as the woman in Picasso's *A Woman Ironing*.
And this morning, though his eyelids rose at the white
sergeant's use of "Stokely" and "Rap," his head didn't
shift an inch from its gallows angle. In two more months
he would get—*out*, if he didn't get into trouble meanwhile.

Less circumspect was the Negro at Thompson's left.
Although he acted as plain, simple, stereotypical as a
redcap if someone doesn't tip, *Uh, I may be fussed up a
little, but,* he stood up and started asking things. "Uh—
sir? Usually in these riots you see the poor people, you
don't see the rich people there. Isn't that right, sir?"

"Actually," the lieutenant replied, "you'd be surprised
how many people are communists there."

"Uh—sir?"

"The rest were all 'stilled by Stokely Carmichael," the
sergeant contributed.

"Uh—"

"Sometimes," a Negro put in, "those what has the
authority they all done *cause* the riots. Like the police
hitting a guy upside of the head."

"No one disagree with you there," the lieutenant answered. "Let us go on."

"Uh—sir? When it happened in Watts, how come the gover'ment didn't try to stop the trouble there?" The boy meant, try to improve things.

"Okay," the lieutenant said. He was pleased that the GIs were interested in CROWD CHARACTERISTICS—yet he had to get into COUNTERMEASURES soon, the Army rifles and bayonets, the line, echelon, wedge, and diamond formations, the Army's old tactic of yelling out, *"Bayonet— Bayonet—"* the CS gas in burning and bursting grenades, the M9 portable CS gas disperser guns, the M5 helicopter-attached dispersers, the Army's full riflepower: a last resort. "Okay, if I were president of the United States, I could tell you. But," the lieutenant concluded, "I'm not president of the United States. I'm not as smart as he is. I wish I was."

"Uh—sir?"

"Do you have a— Are you married, soldier?"

"No sir."

"Do you have a girl friend?"

"Yes sir."

"When you have a fight with a girl friend, do you go tell people about it?"

"No, but I—"

"Well! When a governor has some trouble he may tell the President of the United States. But he doesn't go telling you, me, everyone here, and the Russians. All right, gentlemen? Let's go on."

"Now, sir! I'm getting a little sick and tired," a Negro spoke up. "Any time there's a riot, everyone says it is communists. I think it's a bunch of bullshit, communists."

"Gentlemen, let's go on," the lieutenant said, but he couldn't go on, obviously. It just wouldn't do, this calling the Negroes gentlemen, for to these young men in their adolescence, manhood—acquiring it, making all America acknowledge it—*manhood,* that was no frivolous thing, and it wasn't being a man when the Man in his officer pinks and u.s. insignia could pull a Negro against his friends, his family, his innermost soul. To the Negroes, the real issue was *America, am I a man or a slave?*

"Sir," a Negro got up and shouted. "What do you think comes first? Are you a man first or a soldier first?"

"I'm a soldier first."

"But sir! You're not going to be in the Army all your life."

"I'm not?"

"Well, we don't feel about the Army like you do!"

"Like the man say," a second one, "if I've got to go into my hometown, do you seriously think I can turn, throw tear gas, and stick everyone with my bayonet?"

"Soldier, what is your rank?"

"You see it on my arm, man!"

"Well, private! You better do those things or you'll get in trouble!"

"Lieutenant, would you do it?"

"I wouldn't have to! City where I live," Boston, "we don't have riots!"

"I've lived for eighteen years in a hole, lieutenant! But they're my people and man! I just couldn't do it!" Disobedience! The soldier riding right into the jaws of treason, "I'd likely end up on their side!"

"*Sir,*" a GI with white epidermis taking the floor. "If they," the Negroes, "if they are so narrow-minded, if they don't have the sense to do the job like they're supposed to—sir, they shouldn't be in the Army."

"*All right, lieutenant. Take your seat.*"
From the wide-awake auditorium, there came a voice that lay on its owner's stomach like a calm saint bernard on a scatter rug. Yet the Colonel who strolled to the rostrum was in time's little nick—as though a red light from an IBM mutiny apprehension console (MAC or "Mac" to the pale specialists who superintended it) had alerted him at battalion scant seconds earlier. "Gentlemen," the Colonel said, the Negroes and whites quieting down, the lieutenant shrinking like Caliban into the shadows, "any time a soldier like you, lieutenant, me, moves to a riot situation, it is because we are ordered to by the President of the United States. It isn't for us as soldiers of the lowest rank to try to interpret the President's political motives. Say," the Colonel continued, "that a factory cans tomatoes in a town of twenty-five thousand, and the cans cause twenty-five babies to die. Well, these twenty-five thousand people might get up in arms and go to that factory. But if the President orders us—"

Never does a soldier do— Always is a soldier a— The grammatical mood the Colonel employed was indicative not subjunctive, for "ought to be" should become "is" within military units and every subjunctive should have a bubble's life. *We will attack at 0600— We will win in Vietnam— A scout is trustworthy loyal—*the sentence structure of Army career men appeared to make realism of idealism and God's will of wishful thinking. It was as though to these officers the GIs were nothing but small wooden soldiers, immaculate of autonomy. So the Colonel talked until recess in this optimistic rhetoric ("We will deploy as soldiers, not as political animals")—while the Negroes gave him the courteous silence that GIs tender to any officer of a rank higher than the officer before him. In the darkness, though, the president of their association whispered, "Jim, he jus' don' know the happenings."

"That was a really *outstanding* class," the lieutenant was saying later on. "There were so few people who weren't awake." A spirited start to the riot-suppression instruction, the lieutenant thought.

The sergeant agreed. A soldier since 1950, the sergeant had an American eagle's nose, and eyes in sockets as dark as cardboard mailing tubes. Reds in Germany, whites in Carolina, anarchists in Honshu, college students in Florida who kept kicking sand at the sightseers in paisley-shaped glasses and saying, *"Screw you,"* seventeen were the riots inside which the sergeant had stood immovably as bricks, bottles, bicycle chains, two-by-fours, and Coke cans hit his white helmet and epithets from *"Niggerlover"* to " 政府の犬 " flew at his purple ears. As seen through the mailing tubes, all questions of are these rioters right or aren't they? all disappeared like mayflies to his vision's periphery, and the rioters all became—*rioters! rioters! ils ne passeront pas!* To his good soldier's way of seeing things, an order to engage the enemy could be no more "unethical" than one on Sunday's puzzle page to play and to mate in three moves. To ask oneself, but is the black king a bad king? was meaningless—*bad* was when white is derelict, when it plays and it fails miserably. A man-machine, the sergeant's rule was to get your assignment and do it: win, whatever, shoot the Pope. He wouldn't scruple to practice what he preached when he told these soldiers one day, "You may be fighting your family. *It can happen,*" an order's an order's an order: obey. To this loyal sergeant, an Army of pickers and choosers, of coteries of colonels or of social associations whose "Yes"s and "No"s lie between the President's orders and their execution—this was unthinkable. He therefore didn't think of it.

He had work ahead, though, for he was aware that the GIs felt, *We are men,* and if a riot started might be a bit—well, overenthusiastic. He was afraid that the GIs were raised on a formula of "Take it and dish it out double, *pow,*" and afraid the same syrup of grit, gumption, ginger, oats, adrenalin, piss, and vinegar might run in their arteries that ran in those national guardsmen in

Newark. *Nemo me impune lacessit*—if anyone threw a Coke can at those guardsmen he got back seventeen billion ergs of potassium nitrate, if anyone put a SOUL BROTHER sign in his window he got rattatat-tat. "We won't do that. If we don't have to," the lieutenant insisted—the sergeant agreed, he thought that he must teach the GIs to cool it, *company, whoa,* his command must be. So one afternoon, he got them together outside the barracks to inculcate christian patience. An oak overhead, the company's couple of hippies high on Doriden, the others all in a May-day mood, it was glory be—a good audience.

"Gentlemen," the sergeant said, the GIs in semicircles around him, listening, "a rioter, the first place he usually stops is a liquor store—"

"Yay," someone interrupted.

"—a gun store a drugstore. What is he looking for in a drugstore?"

"Prophylactics!"

"Dope," a Negro soldier cried.

"Correct," the sergeant continued. "He isn't there to get soda pop. Now, if you observe a man running out of a store with a box in his hands, what do you do?"

"Ta-ta-ta-ta," a GI shouted.

"No," the sergeant corrected him. "Do not fire."

"Not even up in the air?"

"No, you're not in some foreign country," the sergeant continued. "Up in Detroit a national guardsman shot and killed a twelve-year-old Negro boy—"

"Goddam," a Negro soldier said.

"—who was carrying home a television set that his mother had just purchased."

"I would of *started* a riot, sergeant," the Negro declared.

"Roger, that is what starts riots," the sergeant agreed. "But if you're sent to a city, you'll get an instruction on when where whether to fire. If you see some idiot doing one of *these,* one of *these,*" gestures, the sergeant's fingers as fluid as any deaf-and-dumb man's or Stokowski's, the GIs all giggling, "ignore it. Don't tell him, 'You stupid cocksucker, beat it.' Don't take a blank, stick it in, say, 'Sonofabitch, move,' and fire it." The boys laughing, the sergeant cried now, "The national guard did, in Detroit," and he called on a PFC, a white boy, to answer a hypothetical question. "You're in a vehicle. Up comes a character saying, 'You're nothing but a man in a monkey suit—'"

"Amen," a Negro interrupted.

"—he makes a couple obscene remarks and he spits at you. What do you do?"

"Spit at him back," someone suggested.

"Call in artillery."

"Now seriously. What do you do?"

"It depends who he spits on, sergeant," the PFC said.

"He spits on *you,* troop."

"His ass is out."

"What?"

"His ass is—*out,* sergeant. I'm going to beat his goddam head in."

"No," the sergeant corrected him, "no physical stuff is authorized. What you do is you wipe it off."

"*Ohhh.*" A low moan of disbelief arose from the soldiers—from the Negroes too! "I'd throw that vehicle in drive, Jim," a Negro whispered. "I'd go right over him!"

"Uh," grunted another with an eloquent stomp.

"That is the last he gonna spit!" A surprise—the Negro not only would fight, he would fight like the Gangbusters to get some manhood in a society where he must double his fists to practice the only manly art. "Sergeant," the boy interrupted. "Now what would *you* do?"

". . . ," the good sergeant answered. He didn't say a word as his handkerchief passed in pantomime over him.

"*Ohhh,*" another incredulous groan.

"I would do as I was told and do nothing," the sergeant said. "I wouldn't be justified in getting from the jeep and kicking him in the balls. Or getting him in—"

"But sergeant," a Negro said. "Sometimes isn't it good to deliver judgment yourself?"

"No, it is not."

"I would say, 'Get in the vehicle, please,'" a white soldier contributed, "and I would take him around the corner and—"

"Sergeant, we give him a bit of knuckle drill," the Negro again, "he gonna go tell his people that we ain't bullshitting!"

"You men aren't getting the point," the sergeant exclaimed. "You aren't supposed to *incite* a riot."

"What if he pisses on you, sergeant?"

"Let us move on. Snipers," the sergeant said to a white boy. "You're taking sniper fire, so what should you do? Ready on the right, ready on the left, ready on the firing line? Open a barrage of fire?"

"No! I'd kill him myself!"

"No," the sergeant insisted. "First of all take cover—"

"And then! Drop in M-seventy-nines," someone cried.

"A four-point-deuce mortar would do!"

"A one-fifty-five!"

"Gentlemen! You're not in Vietnam! These are American people! *You—will—not—*" the sergeant went on, still using the Army indicative although it was clearly contrary to fact—*"at no time use a weapon without authority."*

The soldiers dissented. A man must acquit himself if someone tosses a bottle, hollers, "Up your bright rosy red," erects his right middle finger, or fires a Remington rifle. "What do we do? Lie there and die? I *won't*," a white boy—a staff sergeant—shouted.

"Gentlemen. Gentlemen," the sergeant said. "You've got to (and I don't know how to instill this in you)—you've got to keep control of your faculties. Or you're not a damn bit better than the people you're up against."

"Do you mean, sergeant," a Negro jeered, "we have to stand there and take it?" The question was a rhetorical one—the Negro's eyes had an answer to it, *Unthinkable, am I a man or a mouse?*

The soul brothers had a dilemma, evidently. Like the Negroes who didn't fit on Madison avenue, the Negroes here seesawed between the *too little* and the *too much.* "We are men," they kept saying—but a man's conscience insisted don't be America's slave, and a man's unconscious answered don't be a conscience-stricken mouse. If there was a riot, it wasn't clear what the Negroes would do if ordered to go. Not do it? Or *overdo* it? A real dilemma— either way, it now occurred to the sergeant that he didn't have an Army but merely a crowd—a *crowd*—of some willful people, that the Negro opinions of "We are men" were right in his strategy's way. The rack, psychology, KP, lobotomy—nothing, short of just shooting them he could do nothing about it. "I'm telling—I'm telling you what you ought to do," the sergeant conceded. "I'm not telling you what you're going to do." And that answer tore the tissue of Army grammar apart like a lottery ticket that had lost.

No matter. The consummation of all this wouldn't be in Newark but at the brown barracks itself. One afternoon soon, the GIs would become actors and do a make-believe riot at their athletic field, a riot officially called an exercise or an "X." Imitation rioters would cry, "Up against the wall, motherfuckers," the GIs would fall in, forward march, and be as irreproachable as boys whose shining rifles and bayonets were on puppet strings held by a sergeant: anyhow, so the scenario went. The exercise or "X" was the crucial test for the Army: still, it was astonishing how many $1,000's and $1,000's the

Army was flinging left and right for realism's sake—an Army, remember, that had been niggardly until now. Nothing but a cold auditorium, no microphones, invisible visual aids, an electric light in whose uncompromising rays the sergeant seemed like a Zoroastrian icon of man's duality, half of his face radiant, the other half in black shadow—this, and suddenly the Army was acting like MGM as it plunged its unallocated funds into a thousand ells of sized canvas cloth for a set inside which the GIs could have an "X" with verisimilitude. Two blocks long, two stories high, the Hollywood set's authenticity shone like a Tiffany diamond from the MERRY MARIE'S CAFE and JP'S SECOND-RATE FURNITURE and JAKE'S RECREATION HALL and SLEEZY JOE'S ROOMS 25¢ A NIGHT. Boop boop adoo, it was second best to busing them all to Newark itself. Of course, there was a reason for it. A real lieutenant general would be in Georgia, and therefore the extravaganza. "Now, nothing unusual," the general said, was the man serious?

Anyhow, the soldiers had a scenario thirty-eight pages long, and the "X" would go according to script, "The sniper is bent slightly forward, coughing, choking, rubbing his eyes . . ." Not only GIs but MPs, Georgia police, and firemen would put in some guest appearances, and in late afternoon a $100,000 helicopter would add a high third dimension to the riot below. Fifty-caliber ball ammunition would— *As you were,* there would be only cardboard blanks and a CS substitute that the "rioters" could bear. With half of the GIs playing rioters, the others went to the athletic field every day to learn how to terrify them by step! stomp! by marching against them in a line, echelon, wedge, or diamond, bayonets high. "If you do a bayonet movement," a lieutenant fresh out of OCS taught, "give a vicious growl to instill a fearing instinct in the individual in front of it. Right? Right," the lieutenant taught as the squads learned the bayonet's wild repertory. *"Safeguard. On guard,"* Thompson cried, Thompson being a sergeant. *"Squad of squirmishers— move."*

"Skirmishers," the lieutenant corrected him.

"Squad of squirmishers—move!" Thompson repeated, his squad stepping and stomping forward.

All eyes behind yellow celluloid, all ambiguities of attitude behind rubber masks, the GIs would look at the general with as awe-inspiring faces as African mandrills. No less prepossessing would be the GIs in Levi's, their fingers around the "Molotov cocktails" or the styrofoam stones or the picket signs saying BURN THE MAYOR. Many of these "rioters" would be Negroes with the Stanislav-skian advantage of a life which anticipated art, for many were rioters prior to the President's greeting them. One had once hurled his Molotovs, his boiling water, and his swearwords down at GIs under the Colonel's own com-mand: three died, a coincidence that was revealed when the riot sergeant asked one day, "Has any member of this group been a member of a mob?"

"I'm going to tell him," the Negro had whispered as white soldiers rose to confess to their wildest oats—a panty raid at Maryland, whatever. "Mine," he announced when the sergeant had recognized him, "Mine was the one when they had the—ahem, the little misunderstanding in Panama."

"What side were you on?"

"Well, the Panamanian, sergeant. I'm a Panamanian citizen. Now it surprises me," he went on ambiguously, "it surprises me to see me on America's side." He didn't say if *being* or *being seen as* an American had surprised him—a change of heart or a change of clothes. A difference, obviously, though the sergeant thought that the Negro meant, "I at last pledge allegiance to—" and many white soldiers applauded.

Thompson now, Thompson had been arrested in Dunn seventy-two times—yet it wouldn't matter much at "X" hour. Negroes at either end of the bayonets just had to remember, *Don't adlib,* and an "X" as perfect as *Sugarfoot* would play to the general—a captain with a bullhorn shouting, "In the name of the governor, disperse," a Stokely of sorts replying, "Hell, no! We won't go," a troop of *Papio sphinxes* appearing and Thompson telling them, "Squirmishers, move," an Army band rendering, *One dark night*—

> *A hot time*
> *In the old town*
> *Tonight.*

As the saying goes, *Deo volente,* though it turned a man's brain to tapioca to contemplate what the general would say of it. Would the general slap his swagger stick on his pinks, exclaiming, "A-one typical riot training, gentlemen! Tip-top!" Or would the general turn the color of Bavarian blaukraut and cry, "Schweinen! What do you think of me? I wanted it typical!" When the "X" had ended, when the mayor and the captain had shaken hands at Cinecittà center, when the Army's literal brass had struck up *Happy days are here again,* would the GIs have a black eye or a feather in their service cap? History will never tell us, because—

WE INTERRUPT THIS FOR A BULLETIN! *"Dr. Martin Luther King was shot tonight and is in critical condition in a Memphis hospital. He was on the balcony—"*

At a club where soldiers had Buds while the television movies hummed—hummed—*Now you belong to Broadway*—hummed, from the TV they suddenly heard the hard jarring cough of reality. It was as though a patient, gray, a month in a coma, inaudibly breathing, all hope abandoned, ignored, had twisted and suddenly spit up a glutinous ball of blood. *"The shot, apparently—"*

"One down," a boy at the club chortled at NBC's news. "And one less to go."

"P . . . too! Right through the neck," another.

"I got a riddle," another. "What is a Mrs. Martin Luther King?"

"I give up. What?"

"She is—*a black widow!* Ha!"

"Ha!"

"Excuse me," a Negro at the next table interrupted. "Do you think this is funny?"

"I think it is funny."

"Show me how funny it is."

And the rumble began! With a violence out of TV movies—the tables overturning, the chairs in the air like falling axes, the crash! of a Coke bottle breaking, edges as sharp as a raven's call and as sharp as a tuttle-tooth saw. The searchlights and siren sounds of MPs approaching—cool it! cheese it! rendezvous later at club number two! Negroes were on a rampage tonight at a camp across the Appalachians, in Kentucky.

We interrupt this for a bulletin! At the brown barracks in Georgia, the hands of a Negro flew to his eyes as though they'd been hit by caustic soda. *Oh,* the mild-mannered soldier thought. *It's going to happen now.*

"Goddammit," a white soldier asked him. "Why do they keep interrupting? Who is Martin Luther King?"

"He a leader of colored people."

"Hell then! He needed be killed!"

"No, he believe in nonviolence. He—we thought he would be the first colored president."

"Bullshit," the white soldier teased him.

We interrupt this for a bulletin! "Hey, Thompson! Hey, Thompson, the Man is dead!"

Was it hours? was it months? was it centuries? later, that the GIs were pitching tents in a park of six hundred acres in Baltimore, Maryland? Day and night, the Captain had cried contradictory orders, "Out to the airstrip!" "Back to the barracks!" *"Dress right dress and cover down—forty inches all aroun'!"* "Out to the airstrip!" "Up to Washington!" "Up to Baltimore, everyone!" Yet one couldn't say of this company that it had *traveled* to Baltimore—it had been carefully lifted by a nurse, perhaps, and Baltimore had been slipped underneath it like a little bedpan. Not a whit of GI life had changed, though the vista had. The five o'clock reveille, the breakfast line, the "SOS" of warm chipped beef on lukewarm toast, the morning walk to clear the vicinity of cigarette stubs, the details—here in a Baltimore park the GIs kept to their ways at a far remove from the city's towers of smoke or the fire, police, ambulance sirens that all spiraled around like the seagulls around the smokestacks of sanitation scows. Here beneath a Druid tree the Negroes sat whispering, "Hit 'em, Ben," playing craps, the quarters skipping from boy to boy to boy like cricket frogs, while at another tree the white soldiers—pinochle, or they fiddled at sticking the trees with a bayonet. "Living is hard, isn't it," Thompson said ironically. "Well, this is what love of country do for us," *love of country* being the battalion motto.

For the GIs were still standing to—standing by. Sooner or later, when the first sergeant blew on a whistle and ordered them, "Fall in," saddle up, helmets on, mount bayonets—at that ultimatum, the Negroes and whites would rejoin reality. In the interim—Baltimore!

Now and again, the GIs wondered, "Which is the best whorehouse?" "Will the Orioles play?" One of the Negroes had family here: an aunt, uncle, teenager cousins, the riot sergeant's wife had a sister who visited him, "How are you, honey," a Negro had a mother he hadn't seen for years, "I don't believe it," "It's true." Baltimore! Not an hour's drive away was the University of Maryland, the school of the second lieutenant whose riot was a panty raid. *If only,* the lieutenant thought now. Friday and Saturday there would be drunken orgies at his fraternity house, this the lieutenant was sure of. If he could only be there! Hee—haw, rum in a Coke, rye in a ginger, piss in a pilsner glass and pass it around. "Have a beer on Sigma Chi," "It's a little warm," "We've run out of ice." Bright college years.

> *Sigma Chi! Sigma Chi!*
> *We're the boys who satisfy . . . yi yi.*
> *Richer, longer lasting too,*
> *We're the boys with super woo . . . oo oo.*

Nostalgic, the lieutenant thought of the coeds on the frat-house carpet, their legs up under their red wool skirts.

> *We want to make you!*
> *We want to make you!*
> *We want to make you laugh and cry . . . yi yi.*

All the girls giggling at "make you," their fingers in front of their mouths meaning, *I am a proper lady,* but also meaning, *I understand,* cars in the parking lot rock-

ing, stockingless legs out of slotted tops of Renaults—
Rrrr! And a whistle blew in Baltimore, the first sergeant
hollered, "Fall in!"

It worked like a snap! at the eyes of the hypnotized.
Awake, and with "Yahoo"s and "Hooha"s the white
soldiers threw the footballs into the fourth dimension,
virtually sprinting in. *"Lessgo," "Andiamo," "Didi,"*
the white soldiers shouted, *"Didi"* meaning "Go go" in
Vietnamese. Bored! is what the Caucasians had been—as
bored as they'd been in Vietnam after walking, walking,
shooting at people's pigs. Nor were the whites given
pause by the possible irony of fighting for America one
month and fighting inside it the next one. No—a GI's
near neighborhood of Army green cotton togs, Army
yellow PFC stripes, Army other enlisted men, Army
tents, weapons, messkits, canteen cups, and C-ration cans
—a GI's environment in the paddies and in Baltimore's
parks didn't fluctuate except in degrees of Fahrenheit.
Inevitably, Army pink plastic teaspoons peeped like Kil-
roy from the shirt pockets of GIs camping in Asia tonight
and GIs falling in ranks today to march on the crab-cake
state. Nor, in principle, would the Army's mission this
day be anything new to Vietnam's veterans. "We military
men are in Vietnam now—" in Vietnam, if you didn't
carry this in your wallet you might have a stripe taken
from you—"because its government asked us to help it,"
cross out *Vietnam,* write in *Maryland,* and it still applied:
the settlers of Baltimore were under attack, the Army's
the cavalry.

Asia and America, the white soldiers saw as their enemies the same ubiquitous badmen—the communists. The thinking went in Vietnam:

1. We are killing them.
2. If they aren't communists, what are we doing killing them?
3. So they're communists,

and logic accommodated itself to military necessity in Baltimore, too. "Are they drunk?" "Do they think they're better than us?" *"I know, they're communists,"* the white soldiers here in Baltimore had these—hardly thoughts, for they weren't the outcome of mental labor but a desperate input to spare mental labor, the alibis for an absent intelligence. The saints can indulge in empathy with the enemy, but if GIs are asked to be Hamlets and to go through mental agonies to get to moral uncertainties—well, the GIs will say, "What is in it for us?" In war, the GIs were without consciences, really—even in Georgia, at the sight of SLEEZY JOE'S ROOMS the GIs who weren't black had just chuckled condescendingly at such unpresentable digs. And getting to Baltimore in Army trucks, they had had fun and yelled at the Negroes there, "White power!"

Of course, the soul brothers knew the ghetto better. But if the ghost of King had been looking at Baltimore as the first sergeant said, "Fall in," and those existential questions *am I a man or a slave? a man or a mouse?* demanded immediate answers—if King had been watching, he may have wondered what the brothers were up to.

No one outdistanced the Negroes in shaking their legs and in getting going to Baltimore. "That is a whistle, gentlemen! That ain't no bird, gentlemen! *Lessgo,*" Thompson cried, and the president of the soul brothers association sprinted in.

"Company," the first sergeant cried when it had formed ranks. "*Attention.* Dress right—*dress.* Ready—*front.*"

"Okay," the Captain began. "We are having a little hot water downtown. The cause—the cause is people handing out weapons. We got those national guard guys, and I'm telling you—" *I'm telling you,* anywhere in America a captain's a captain—"they're like a bunch of bums, their hands in their pockets and their shoulders scrunched. You men, I want you to look like soldiers. I don't want you lounging around. I don't want you smoking cigarettes. I don't—"

"It's a goddam beauty contest," a white boy whispered.

"I don't want you in grimy fatigues," the Captain concluded. "People lose all their respec' for you."

"You heard the man," the first sergeant hollered now. "Let me see clean fatigues. Let me see those boots—*shine,* or I'll restrict you, everyone go without you."

"I'm going to cry," a white boy whispered.

"Fall in again in fifteen minutes. *Fall out,*" the first sergeant ordered.

It was harassment again. But what wasn't? and with their usual animadversions the Army's white slaves fell out to their duffel bags for a change of clothes. "Got to put on clean fatigues to have people throw shit," "Oh, you're going to hate yourself if you're shot," "It's a real honor to go," Caucasians in underwear grumbled. But the Negroes—the Negroes did enthusiastically what the Army wanted them to. One, afraid that he might be left behind, said, "Lieutenant, I got no other fatigues."

"So whose fault is that?"

"The Army's! They don't pay me," the Negro insisted —the gospel truth. He was being gypped by an IBM error of half a year's obstinacy.

"Sorry about that," the lieutenant said.

"Sir, it just don't make sense," the Negro kept on, brokenhearted. He wanted to go, although he had cousins in Baltimore and although in Georgia he had once sworn, "I'll never go." He sat down outside his puptent with the Baltimore blues.

"What," a white soldier argued, "what, if you don't go you'll be on KP?"

"They don't want me to go I won't go," the Negro pouted. "Hey," he said suddenly. "Do you have extra fatigues?"

"Here. But they're from Korea."

"Hey sir," the Negro cried now. "I got a shirt, but it ain't got no proper patch," instead of a Georgia bayonet it had a black hourglass, the symbol of a unit by T-bone hill.

"It ain't going to pass. It—*look*," the lieutenant told him, "I don't care if you wear it as long as I don't hear about it."

"Thank you, lieutenant, sir!" And the soldier ran to his tent again for a riot rifle, a bayonet, and a pen to write F—A—etcetera, his family name, in big black letters over the pocket, where it wouldn't go unseen.

"Sir, do I look like I need a shave?" Thompson asked.

"You're okay," the lieutenant answered.

"I know I shaved this morning," Thompson said delightedly.

"Fall in," the first sergeant hollered again—and as bright and as Rinso-white as a wooden-soldier set, the Negroes passed muster. Now they would march on Baltimore—

To ravage it? To say, "You stupid cocksucker, beat it"? To use rifles, grenades, and machine guns on it? Another few minutes would tell. "Lessgo," the GIs said while getting on buses showing a CHARTERED in the front windows and a HI-HO YOUR SILVER TO CENTRAL SAVINGS BANK on the sidewalk sides. The buses left looking like—yes, like parochial school ones, the passengers staring at Baltimore, aged, sexed, and dressed alike. What the GIs saw were stately homes: the Tudor homes of stones that one couldn't lift, the Georgian homes of aristocratic brick, the Colonial homes in paint fresh as grade A milk—shinglewood units succeeding them as Negroes appeared at the upper windows. Homes with their balusters broken: this is where there would be trouble, the GIs were told. "Okay! You're going to do what you came here to," a grim sergeant said, as the HI-HO buses started, stopped, and let off GIs, two or three to each corner to defend it. "Now remember! You're only to fire if your life's in danger. That doesn't mean," the sergeant continued, "that if someone's a hundred and fifty yards—" in Vietnam he had said meters—"away, and he calls you a double mother, it doesn't mean you're in danger. You're not in Vietnam," the sergeant concluded. While that was no lie, still it was eerie how Saigonese all of Baltimore seemed as soon as each second drugstore had Georgia men with rifles and Army radios in front of it. "Foamy crest," the GIs were saying, "this is foamy crest two seven alpha. Sitrep negative. Over." The very O_2 of the atmosphere—the very electrons of oxygen ran in elliptical orbits now, jittery, unreliable, ominous, dark, and shadows could even be finger-felt as they could in Vietnam. Every old *Sun* paper blowing out of some alleyway whispered, *Anything can happen now.* And yet, the white boys in Baltimore stayed cool, the white boys in Baltimore were everything that the Army desired. "I'm sorry to bother you, sir. I'll have to see some identification—"

And the Negroes? Men without passion, no one outshone the Negroes in self-control. "I'm sorry to bother you!" "Sorry to trouble you!" "Sorry—" a Negro from the city gangs behaved like a mousy washroom attendant full of endless apologies. Another just smiled when a man with a fistful of bullets came up, "I'm coming back later, and I got something to put them in." *Shoot,* the boy thought imperturbably, *he just a no-good hoodlum, nothing more.* In a whiter part of Baltimore, at a shopping center where he was standing guard at Hollywood's *How to Save a Marriage,* Thompson was truly a Como of emotional cool. He didn't fire at double mothers or take spitters around the corner *and,* he just spoke into his Army radio, "A civilian man? He said he would be back later to kill us?"

"Tsss! Give him a spray of CS," said a white boy.

"No," Thompson chided him. "Not under no condition. Well, under one condition. That when I'm ordered to by my commanding officer—" Hey, President Thompson! What in Stokely's sweet name are the Negroes up to?

THE SECRET OF VANTEE THOMPSON. *Born on March 17, 1946, in Philadelphia, Pennsylvania, or Dunn, North Carolina, one yellow certificate endorsing each. Zodiac sign Pisces, the night mansion of Jupiter. Male. The baby weighed six pounds, two ounces, avoirdupois, or three pounds, eight ounces, if counted as just three-fifths of a person. "Wah," he said, and he drank mother's milk, the calcium precipitating in his wobbly bones. Bare minutes old, he felt the miraculous process of God and environment making a boy a man.*

Smoke Camels! A man's cigarette! Buy a Packard— be the man who owns one! Read Esquire! The magazine for men! For twenty-one years, from TV tubes, transistor radios, from the PA-amplified lips of Gary, Errol, Charlton, Marlon, and Lee, the bells of four-button telephones, snaps of attaché cases, tires of Ferraris cornering, America cried at Thompson its criteria of what he should be. But duplicitously, America said, "Now, don't be a six-pound weakling, Vantee. Be a man instead," and *"Negro, you had better not."* Up in the balcony with you. Go around to the kitchen door. Be the last at the 'bacca farm to drink from the gallon jug.

"Boy! You don't be drinking no water afore us."

"How come?"

"Because you is colored people."

Seventeen—we must forgive him if T-for-Tantalus tried to use force to acquire the forbidden fruit. "Vantee," the Negro football captain asked him. "You any nerve?"

"What do you mean nerve?"

"You man enough to do what I do?"

"I'm as crazy as you are!"

"All right. *Two tickets, please,*" the tackle said at the movie theater in Dunn. But he didn't trudge to the balcony like a kid to bed when company comes, he plunked himself where the Man sat contentedly, and Thompson did too. Kumbaya! the very first sit-in in North Carolina. Like a candle caught in a cold draft, the movie died and Marilyn said, "Kiss me, darl—" or something, and nothing more. The house lights rose, and "Boys," said the skinny theater owner. "You don't allowed to sit here." But soon they had thirty uppity colored people beside them.

The policemen came. "Vantee," a Negro one asked him. "What you doing here in this mess?"

"I'm a leader of men," Thompson answered. "And this is where the men are."

"You know I got to take you downtown."

"Well," Thompson smiled. "We on our way then." Guilty, Thompson was given two days in Dunn's cellar jail, for lying in front of a Trailway he got another twelve later, for picketing at Piggly Wiggly— By now, a hundred and sixty kids were in prison with him, it looked like a slaver ship as they chanted,

I want to be treated like a man,
  Oh yeah!
I want to be treated like a man,
  Oh yeah!
If this ol' Mr. Charlie would just treat me like a man,
Then this would be a great ol' lan',
  Oh yeah!

Yet as Thompson added his *"Yeah"*'s to the tackle's impromptu lyrics, it was interesting that he didn't remember that he couldn't overcome this way. "The white man, he usin' every tech' on us," Thompson's old grandfather taught him—it was true, the white people used a lasso that the harder he fought to free himself from, the tighter it drew around him: he was just getting tied to the white people's formula for an American man. Admit it: nothing in human anatomy decreed that to sit in a balcony is something unworthy—no, British kings and Lincoln did it, orchestra seats in other years were the ghettos of the general. The front and back of buses get to

Raleigh concurrently, nor do male hormones lie in Camels or Cadillacs or the white man's money—the Kalahari of Africa and the Christians say otherwise. It was saner if Thompson now sought in some other frame of reference, but if some other culture spoke from out of his chromosomes he had scarcely heard it. *I want to be treated like a man*—he had fought free of the frying pan to get into something worse: he was stuck in America's definitions.

A *man*. A boy became one by belonging to something whose thump was a thousand times that of his unassisted heart. To fit, though, he had to rid himself of everything that the machinery couldn't absorb—of everything in him that wasn't immaculate fact. To fit, he didn't grow, he shriveled—he cut, he chiseled, he amputated himself like the poor *bikari,* the beggars in India who acknowledge that men do better without their legs. To be himself and to love, to hate, to laugh, to cry, to hope, to fear, to make every minute of life something real, to feel—or to refrain in all conscience, sometimes, these an American man didn't do, a man just abandoned the unassimilable. Of his psyche's three parts, he discarded unconscious, *am I a man or a mouse,* discarded conscience, *am I a man or a slave,* he shrank instead into the Freudian ego, a scrap of cool, controlled, calm intellect that he fitted without any friction into America's wheelworks. He became brass, the cold residue when he was stripped of all that's spontaneous—of all that's alive, he got rigor mortis to get himself with it, to fit himself in, to—

Fall in. The first sergeant's words were in Thompson's ears. His world like a wet rose opening, like a white woman yielding, like its petals her pale thighs parting, *enter me*—America was saying what a man must be and letting him be it! At last, Thompson was someone at America's center, king of America's sidewalk, cop on America's corner: the Man. It was true, little that he could do in Baltimore went to advance the colored people —the colored were called the "Boons" at this shopping center and in a year would still be. Thompson himself, in twelve months would be a *"Boy"* in a Newark paint plant, a scar on his hand where a baling press in a box factory smashed it, red in his eyes where acid in a bumper factory splashed it, his wife separated, his telephone disconnected, his baby miscarried, his car repossessed, the Army itself billing him—a cheap barbecue on his dinner plate. All in a year: today, though, we must excuse him if being a man appeared irresistible and if being a man meant being dead.

"Two seven. Two seven," Thompson was saying into his Army radio. "Two seven. Say again?" Yesterday, out of C-ration carton wire he had fashioned sort of an earmuff to attach a black telephone to, "Convenient. I can easily hear," he had reported in Baltimore's empty park. But at Baltimore's new white shopping center—*caw*. America stood like a palisade around him, electromagnetic waves from the Army's two-seven element ran up against the packed racks and the overflowing counters, and like soldiers up to their shoulders in Asia's mud were robbed of all their vitality—and *caw*. A thousand yards of fluorescent tubes set up electric echoes in Thompson's ear. "Lieutenant—" he turned to the sigma chi—"I'm sitting in a canyon, sir."

"You've got it on the freq?"

"Affirmative." With his old Asia hands he screwed in a ten-foot aerial such as the long-range reconnaissance people use. "Two seven! Say again," he requested, the aerial leaning over Baltimore like a palm tree. "Two seven— *What? What? Lieutenant,*" he cried excitedly. *"We done made contact!"* Meaning, let the bugles blow! the enemy's been met.

And as GIs say, it was hairy. So hairy that the Colonel, Kentucky born, crewcut, built like a wooden shipping crate—the Colonel was there, fatigues on, firelight on his right-angled jaw. The site was a grocery out of whose window a diffident arm of fire gestured like a lone clerk calling help—the fire was a one-alarmer, merely, though as leaves are drawn to a holocaust the Negroes had felt themselves drawn to this little pathetic fire. By now, three concentric circles of men were standing around it. Red, green, and black: in the innermost circle, the Baltimore fire department put forty pounds of water pressure onto the grocery, back to back against them the Army's squad of skirmishers was "On guard," and its bayonets were at the Negroes in the outermost circle. "A bayonet. There is nothing like it," the sergeant had taught everyone, "in the beautiful sunshine for psychological effect," it just wasn't so today, though. "Out of our neighborhood, you—" obscenities, the Negro women went up against the bayonets shouting this, and the Negro men issued oceans of human uncertainty into the System.

"You silly motherfuckers," a Negro shouted. "Out in the alleyway playing army."

"At least we aren't rioting," a PFC—a white one— whispered.

"Shut up, bitch! You short fat faggot," the Negro answered, his beard like a chisel against the air. "You fat redheaded—" etcetera, his finger against a bare bayonet. He suddenly caught at a GI's rifle.

"Don't let 'em take it," a lieutenant cried. And horizontal butt-stroke—*crack,* the GI set the wooden end of his rifle around like a right to the jaw.

"You hit me," the Negro screamed and— Nothing. No one in the concentric circles moved. For the moment, centrifugence and centripetence evened out.

In his jeep parked close to the focus of forces, the Colonel looked on. *Anything can happen,* the Colonel thought—in the skirmish line, he had seen three of the soul brothers shoulder to shoulder, and to their vulnerable ears the Negro was now addressing himself. Forces and forces must tug at these boys, the Colonel suspected. "Man, I just couldn't do it," a Negro had blurted in Georgia's dark auditorium. "Give him a bit of knuckle drill," another had cried another day. "I will carry out orders," a plastic card in every boy's right breast pocket said, and in Army indicative and in fierce capital letters it continued:

1. *I will* PRESENT *a* NEAT APPEARANCE . . .
2. *I will* BE COURTEOUS WITH CIVILIANS . . .
3. *I will* NOT FIRE *my weapon* EXCEPT . . .

I will—I will—I will— *But will they?* the Colonel thought, while the Negro with the goatee implored them, "Why are you with the white trash? Come on over to our side! Come on—" Would the Negroes choose to go over? overreact? hold on? *Anything can happen*, the Colonel thought.

And as the minutes passed and as chitterlings, trotters, tails put a few last ounces of fuel on the dying fire, the Colonel saw that the Negroes were standing fast. And well they might, the Negroes were doing nothing in Baltimore they weren't already doing to themselves. In the crunch, the soul brothers were as that sergeant said— as loyal, as cool, as sergeants themselves, as Negro policemen in Dunn, North Carolina, as wheels within wheels, as Senegalese *tirailleurs* in Africa, *absolument,* as infantrymen in Vietnam. Tell the Negroes to fix their bayonets, do a vertical butt-stroke, put in a bullet, shoot—tell the Negroes to kill someone, and the Negroes would do it. Or tell the Negroes don't and they won't—*outstanding,* the Colonel told himself. *They are good soldiers, the Negroes. They are good men.*

6 /

A day later—call me mister, please, a boy in the soul association got out. "Our congratulations," a form letter from the U.S. government told him. "And thanks for the service rendered. In reply refer to 328/231—" A piece of paper, the Negro thought, he forgot it and flew to Chicago to the plastic roses, plastic lemons, plastic antimacassars, and a plastic sphere with a Christ in it— to the gold-covered fireplace logs of his mother's home. To her hearty welcome.

He went to the railroad yard to ask about being an Oiler again. En route in a Pontiac, his cousin, a redcap, sat alongside to orient him to Chicago's new configurations, the outcome of its own recent riot. "And that was an A&P, remember? And that was an apartment house," the cousin declared. "A shame inside of another shame!" At the railroad yard, the overflow oil on the rails, stones, dandelions, oil on the sparrows, apparently, a man in white shirt sleeves met the Negro, telling him, "Well! The war's over now! You're coming back, I hope."

"Yeah."

"And you were a Helper?"

"I was an Oiler."

"Oh. There was a layoff. I got guys seniorer than you—"

It was something ironic: I may just riot myself, the

Negro thought. To his mind, being a man meant being an Oiler and oiling the wheels which rolled a whole millionth of one percent of America's gross national product, such as plastic antimacassars, to Chicago. If he wasn't part of America—well, the Negro had joked about this to Thompson a few days before, "I be in the streets myself."

"I see you, I give you a horizontal butt-stroke," Thompson had answered him.

"You better come to my side."

"I give you a bayonet up the ass."

As for Thompson, the riot stopped and Thompson's company flew to its fort in Georgia—to the daily harassments of the brown barracks and of the little structure outside it. The latter looked like a little pissoir but it was a bulletin board that the GIs stood at to learn, among other things, that the cuffs of their trousers should be at least seventeen inches and that their sleeping bags shouldn't be dry cleaned or "Death may result." In particular, the GIs stood there at six every morning to learn the precise sort of foolishness that the Army had ordered them to: say whether to "die" today in a make-believe village, to paddle across to Alabama in tanks, or to help train the German shepherd dogs by falling and playing possum till a PFC whispered, "Good dog," in Fang's pointed ear. One unforgettable morning, the GIs learned from the bulletin board that it had committed them to area seventy-seven.

Seventy-seven! Sunset Strip, the GIs had nicknamed it.

As they got on their canvas-covered trucks, the GIs—mirabile dictu, all really looked forward to seventy-seven, a "Vietnamese" village built of old yellow sticks like a Hollywood set. As with SLEEZY JOE'S ROOMS, *a charitable wish to improve on Vietnam's real villages had led the Army to virtually sterilize this one—for instance, to rake it in ribbons as parallel as the ones cabaña boys put on Miami's beaches at eight every day. No filthy pigs or noisy chickens intruded here: no little children, either, all of the yellow houses were at equal intervals on the periphery, like the teeth of some giant gear. In this village, half of the company would be GIs who would "seal and search" somewhat as they did in Vietnam itself, shouting to a lieutenant and—of vital importance—to a class of officer candidates in the bleachers, too, "It looks suspicious, sir!" "It's a tunnel, sir!" "It's a booby trap, sir!" "It's a spike trap, sir!" "It's ammo, sir!" In quans and in conical hats, the other soldiers would do their bit by being the "Vietnamese" and by squatting around like a tribe of uncooperative apes.*

At one o'clock, it was curtain time. A peal of rip-roaring laughter arose from the officer candidates as GIs came shuffling out of the Vietnamese hovels, "Son of a—" "Look at those goddam guys!" Besides being racially integrated, the "Vietnamese" were indulging in every shameless cliché of TV, some putting their arms in their sleeves like the Chinese and others bowing spasmodically like the Japanese, "Ah so!" Presently, the GIs in combat clothes surrounded the whole mise en scène, and an interpreter with a battery-operated bullhorn cried, "Get out of the houses, everyone," in Spanish. The reason for Spanish was, the Army had learned that the troops couldn't speak any Vietnamese but "Didi" or go away. And wouldn't even try.

"Ah so. Ah so," a lieutenant had prompted them.

"Yackety yackety do," a sergeant suggested.

"Blah blah blah blah," a lieutenant tried. No success— the GIs didn't volunteer, and the sergeant turned to the Panamanian soldier.

"Troop," the exasperated sergeant said. "I don't know if you speak anything but English but you will yak! You will get on the bullhorn and yak!"

Roger dodger. And that afternoon, the "seal and search" started with a GI telling the Vietnamese loudly, "Sal' de la casa, y tiren se al suelo—" It didn't go badly, really. Firm with the VC, fair to the innocent farmers, the GIs were through in just thirty minutes, the only miscue occurring when a boy dropped a smoke grenade and a haystack caught fire. At the curtain call, the officer candidates applauded, and the GIs all exited to the pine trees to warm themselves at some campfires of old dead branches and broken cones—a few soldiers put in C-ration sugar to watch it become molasses or blank ammunition to hear it go pop! pop! pop!

"A real good job," a lieutenant went up and commended them. "Except someone burned the haystack. Well," the lieutenant continued, the GIs forming a U around the smoky fire, the smoke escaping from the U's

open chimney, "well," the lieutenant continued. "It added realism."

The soldiers laughed. "We lucky it wasn't a hooch," a house, a Virginia boy said naughtily.

"Yeah! Whole village go up in smoke, sir," a Carolina boy added.

"GIs burn village," a news headline, a Michigan boy invented.

"Now sir," a Missouri boy. He was speaking in earnest: no question, he told himself, if GIs went through the Vietnamese villages as effeminately as this there would be casualties—lots. "Now sir. Would you really search a village that way? We would be ordered to blow up the motherfucker—to call in air and artillery and we wouldn't have a damn hooch left."

"Affirmative. We would blast it," a Virginia boy agreed.

"Sure," a Florida boy said. "At that motherhunching village, we would get OD matches and some kerosene—poof. A man can see where the Army's been! He can see the smoke behind it!"

"Sir? Isn't that how it is," the Missourian asked.

The lieutenant shrugged. Fair's fair, the show hadn't been in the tradition of Shakespeare but of morality plays: it didn't hold a mirror up to nature, it preached. It hadn't been the Army's message to do as I do but rather to do as I say. Besides, the lieutenant himself hadn't been to Vietnam, and to listen to campfire stories of OD matches, kerosene cans, and villages put to the torch made him a *little diffident, often. He wondered, Are these stories nothing but bluster? Is their ring of truth due to their credibility or to his own credulity? Vietnamese drowned, or Vietnamese thrown out of helicopters, or Vietnamese—children—given a chocolate cookie with a mickey of plastic explosive inside: a man could believe this, it could happen if GIs just carried out in their sergeant's squad the same drastic strategies that the GIs urged on America's army. But many stories in Georgia had been absolutely doozers! Had the Florida soldier done it, really—had he executed nine old Vietnamese farmers at his lieutenant's order? "None of them women, of course," even the GI's hasty disclaimer had almost corroborated him, and he had been lifelike when his fingers went to his freckled brow as though to implore someone and suddenly—flew, to show everyone how a Vietnamese forehead splats. A sergeant here: had he really turned a machine gun on three little girls as they washed an old water buffalo? The sergeant asserted so. "Captain said, 'Cut them down.' I guess," and a tiny twitch of disapproval had shown on the soldier's mouth, "I guess he was oneing up Alpha company's body count." A twitch of a lip: a delicate gesture, the lieutenant couldn't think it was counterfeit when it registered on a crude amateur actor from the morality play. A third soldier—but in every squad the GIs had similar stories. It didn't set right to think of these normal boys in the black shirts of Nazis or in barbarian pelts, but if Vietnam's own little people were the wrench in the war machine and if GIs couldn't redeem them— I believe them, the lieutenant thought.*

The pale smoke rose, the GIs still waiting to get their stories in and using their toes in a shuffle-off-to-Buffalo way to kick extra twigs in the dying fire. "Oh sure. We should go to that village," the Florida boy continued, he was meaning the make-believe one, "and set everything in it on fire. If we show those guys how it really is, Christ! We'll be thrown out of—" He paused. He couldn't think of a military unit the GIs might be thrown out of. And soon after that, the GIs were honorably discharged.

7 / BILL

One fine morning, a Florida boy with sunrise-colored hair was up in Manhattan and walking ever so leisurely by Rockefeller center. A veteran of Vietnam, a killer of ten, twenty, thirty—well, a man doesn't count their noses if they're nothing but Vietnamese—civilians, he wore a brown tweed suit and a matching tweed vest. His shirt was white, and a tie of the same forgettable color as carpets in old hotels or curtains in Rembrandt let everyone learn that it was, indeed, a necktie, without its being obstreperous about it. A conventional young man, a credit card in his wallet identified him as William Calley.

He was walking south on the center stripe of the avenue—there, or a few carefree feet to either side. At ten on this sunny morning, a man might attract attention this way if one million others weren't on the asphalt with him—if they weren't toddling along as though traffic lights were so many christmas ornaments, green and red. At the mayor's order, the street didn't belong to the automobile wheels today—if dirty words didn't belong on the air then surely carbon monoxide didn't, it may have seemed to this original mayor. All automobiles absent, the human beings of Manhattan had the same *freude schöner götterfunken* feeling of joy that generally arose when the lights went out or some other calamity happened: a sense that the Lord had allowed them a few uncharted acres to act spontaneously in. All men became brothers, and they didn't think of the men around them as obstacles—rocks, or as robots they had to say *honk* to. They didn't look at Calley as anything but a normal young man.

Normal normal. He was like sugar in water, he had been dropped in a city street scene but he didn't displace anything: it looked like the same scene with or without him. A common trait, a smile he was seldom without sent a low-medium heat to Calley's near neighborhood to turn every latent contretemps to something that he could assimilate easily. His age was America's median age. His birthplace was in Miami, his last occupation, insurance, he had practiced in Frisco, nor was his year in Asia a warrant that he wasn't normal any more—the chances were, he was just one of ten thousand veterans of Vietnam on this teeming street today. Hip hooray, the GIs had come marching home, the men from those brown barracks in Georgia had already beaten their swords in and were civilians in paint plants, in ammonia plants, at ovens where twenty thousand cans of Heinz condensed mushroom soup hit a temperature of two hundred and fifty degrees, and in New York City's Police Department. To have taken part in our adventures in Vietnam was normal today.

No hurry today. At eleven, Calley walked into the world's tallest building, went up it, Calley put pocket money into an owl-eyed telescope, and—as the children did (Calley was five-foot-four)—he stood on the rail around the telescope, peering in. He looked for a woman sunning herself—no success, he looked at the Statue of Liberty, instead, and he then descended to Longchamps: lunch. At his table, he took cigarettes from his jacket pocket instead of his jockey shorts, an abnormal alternative that he had read about in a book about how to stop smoking, and, as he lit up, he started talking of Asia. Arms, artillery, babies in irrigation ditches, dead—of course not, as all normal boys do he reminisced of his rest-and-recreation week in that fabulous city of Bangkok. "Do you know the Strip? There's supposed to be two hundred thousand girls on it," Calley said to a Vietnam veteran he was eating with.

"Two hundred thousand girls?"

"Two hundred girls in every club, and a thousand clubs. I liked the Rhapsody," Calley went on. "I was with these lieutenants and they didn't like the rock group there. So they took over: the infantry officer played piano, the radar officer drums, the male nurse officer trumpet, though, of course, he was so damn drunk that he couldn't pucker up, the artillery officer guitar. He was just deafening, he was jumping with it and vibrating it, *zzz,* he was even worse when he was strumming it, though, he had never played a guitar before. And they hadn't played

piano, or drums, or trumpets—or anything, so they were
simply making noises and singing songs like,

> *I wanna eat you, baby,*
>   *Cause you're good to eat,*
> *I wanna eat you, baby,*

or dirty lyrics for *Hey Jude,*

> *Hey Jude,*
>   *I wanna eat your box,*
> *Hey Jude—*

the Ugly Americans, if I weren't drunk I'd have thought
they're obnoxious. The radar officer broke one of the
snare drums—he just screamed fuck it and threw it across
the Rhapsody and jumped on the bass drum, too. And
bent one of the cymbals, too."

"And you? Where were you?"

"With those girls," Calley smiled. "In the surveys, I
always saw how the average guy in America was getting
laid—I don't know. Twice every week, and I wasn't getting any of it. A guy had been getting my action every
week, and I thought, *I should make it up.* And here was
the Rhapsody and this atmosphere out of the comics—
I could say, I want you and you and you and you and
you. And they were mine."

"I counted five."

"At ten dollars each. The artillery officer, the male
nurse officer, and I got a Volkswagen bus, and we brought
fifteen girls to the hotel with us. It was really ridiculous—

we couldn't sleep with them and we just pranced around. We played harem."

"Gentlemen!" A waiter came up to Calley's table. "A cocktail?"

"A bloody mary," Calley said.

"A virgin mary," the other said.

"A bloody shame," the waiter observed. He left.

"The next day," Calley went on, "twelve of the girls simply drifted off. The other three, we had dinner at the Ramada and later went to the Cat's Eye. And there was a table of tourist ladies near us: horny bats, all of them watching the Thais we were sitting with and whispering, 'It's revolting.' Until the artillery lieutenant interrupted them all, 'Excuse me. I know we are mixing races here, but the girl you're calling a whore is the prime minister's daughter. She understands every word, and you're making a bad impression upon the Thais.' It was just bullshit, but I say those girls weren't really whores. My own one, I've never met a better one—I think I loved her."

"So finally?"

"So finally? We said goodbye and we returned to Vietnam."

For lunch, Calley had four bloody marys: that's all, he then returned to his pleasure trip on the popular center stripe. A typical tourist, really. Old men, nannies in white attire, window shoppers, sweethearts, sightseers in their shoelace ties—as many as ten thousand people saw Calley now without shrinking into the side streets or thinking what a queer specimen. But men can smile and be villains—psychotic villains, psychiatrists say, and Calley was really here in Manhattan to go to the doctor's to undergo tests to see whether he was stark raving mad. Or why would he kill civilians?

"Bowels?"

"Shit."

"Masturbation?"

"Penis," Calley replied. At midnight, he was still in a city townhouse eating the doctor's sandwiches, associating words. And drawing things like a man with eyes, a nose, a mouth with a Halloween smile, but—an important omission, the doctor knew it was normal, though —no sexual organs, and a woman with a Minoan's breasts and an amphora's hips. And animadverting on sayings such as, "One today is worth two tomorrows," "One swallow doesn't make a summer," and "People in glass houses shouldn't throw stones." In time, the psychiatrist, a man whose small mustache rode on his skin as driftwood does in a sea storm, appearing, disappearing, reappearing, under a hundred wrinkles of worry—a real worrywart, the psychiatrist said to Calley, "Well, I have to pee."

It was after one. A long day for Calley, and saying good night to that careworn man he walked back to his hotel—to his room, bringing with him a few hours' homework. No more inscrutable inkblots, the thing was a list of five hundred easy sentences ("I wish I were dead," etcetera) that the psychiatrist told him to answer true or false to—the answers, the doctor would feed to an IBM machine, and in just milliseconds science would say if Calley was normal or non compos mentis. In medical language, it would print out if Calley was schizophrenic, manic, depressive, psychopathic, psychasthenic, paranoid, hypochondriac, hysteric, or introverted, or ("I like poetry," "I like collecting flowers," "I like *Alice in Wonderland*") if the sheik of that oriental harem was in fact homosexual. All right: Calley slept late, at ten he woke up and pulled on some corduroys and he started in.

"I am a special agent of God."

"False," Calley wrote.

"I like to talk about sex."

"True," Calley wrote.

"I am careful to step over sidewalk cracks."

"False," Calley wrote.

"Someone has it in for me."

"True," Calley not only circled this but he shouted it— a wreath of roses sprouted on Calley's face, and Calley now laughed aloud. Ninety-nine, ninety-eight—like a million men on whose calendars the little kisskisses of *x*'s were, in Georgia he had once counted each day to the great getting out. A year later, it was apparent the Army was down on him—it wouldn't release him, in spite of all precedents he had been practically pickled alive in GI grapefruit juice. And acting like one of psychiatry's malevolent mothers, the Army was trying to prosecute him as the deliberate killer of Vietnamese civilians. A

capital crime, the Army now told everyone, and in this circumstance it wasn't screwy of Calley to see himself on the gallows saying—well, he thought he might shout as the paratroops do, "Airborne!" A far better thing to go dropping dead with a smile on.

"Someone has it in for me."

"True," Calley wrote.

"I believe I am being plotted against."

"True," Calley wrote.

"I am sure I am being talked about."

"True," Calley wrote.

"No one seems to understand me."

"True—"

AROUND AND AROUND THE WHEELS GO. *This patient's test results are suggestive of a serious psychiatric condition. He is suspicious, mistrustful, and irritable. He . . .* Numerically, the IBM readout said Calley was eighty-eight—was totally over the edge of the paranoia scale. On the poppycock scale, a man more aware of particulars would put the IBM well ahead of *The Autobiography of Howard Hughes.* Garbage in, garbage out, he might agree that Calley was without conscience, was without wires to his fellow feeling, and was even inhuman, sure, but Calley was crazy? *Au contraire,* he had killed those men in Vietnam as one more participant on a mission that was as far from being abnormal as his elevator ride up the Empire State. A mission that was as American as mom's cherry pie.

A second lieutenant, he had orders to go three kilometers to an objective along the China sea. At six o'clock in the morning, he had woken up, washed, shaved, combed as though he were merely catching the China-sea commuter bus—Calley had caught a helicopter, actually, at seven-thirty he had jumped off it and started east. No stretches of terra incognita lay in Calley's way this sunshiny day. As efficiently as its farm machines, the organizational genius of America had already ripped every sort of unpredictable obstacle out of those three kilometers —out of those critical hours. Migs, malaria, name it— America had virtually gotten rid of space itself and of time itself, unmercifully skinning them and arranging their bones as six-digit coordinates and as T-plus-tens and T-plus-twenties. Ahead of Calley this morning was nothing but daylight, was nothing that we hadn't fitted into the strategy except— A pity, perhaps, except for five hundred units of Vietnamese people.

A stumbling stone. It was normal for Calley to see those twenty-five tons of organic matter this way—a practical fact of America was that living things were in the way almost everywhere and America knew it. The *raison d'être* of a superstate, after all, was the abolition of all uncertainty, which, alas, was a gas that escaped out of living things as regularly as CO_2. Open, uncontrollable, obedient just to its own imperatives—like a runaway horse, life

157

had a way of slipping reins and of running wild, of up-setting the absolutes and of overloading equations with x's. As engineers knew, its intrusion into the three dimensions was a most perilous one. If straws could fray, if sticks could decay, the little pigs of America used plastic, instead, and they built us a world without surprises—a Masonite world that we could control to its outermost inch and its innermost ounce. Or *could* if we still didn't endure the vestigial presence of Man and of the blots his personal determination introduced into the perfect design—words of Jacques Ellul. And Roderick Seidenberg, "As science advanced, man alone appeared a wayward and unpredictable entity in an otherwise tractable universe. Such a system becomes in time intolerable, and—"

It was normal for Calley to see those unpredictables as the only impediments to the implementation of Duty—to his little contribution to our victory in Vietnam. "GI, gimme cigarette," "GI, gimme chewing gum," "GI—" as the day's operation began, the Vietnamese just would irritate, but as Calley went on they inevitably would be behind him, a blank, a big black box, an unknown at Calley's very back. A few people would be scratching the soil, certainly, a few would be sewing samplers, whatever, but GIs and GIs could testify that a few would mutilate everyone's plans by shooting their guns at Calley and Calley's men—or could testify if they weren't dead. A few such volleys, and Calley's new operation would stop on its grid coordinates like a car with four sudden flats. All because of some human beings—no, nor

would the others cooperate in what systems analysis calls
a Sort:

"Who are the VC?"

"I don't know."

"Who are the VC?"

"I don't know."

Intolerable! To kill those misfits would be the normal
way to incorporate them in the strategy, as Calley by now
understood. To act like fairyfolk, to put them to sleep
temporarily with BZ gas was considerate, certainly, but
it wasn't issued to Calley, it was against the Geneva Con-
vention. Having no extra men, he didn't have the option
of guarding these guys or of moving them to the con-
centration camps, and at this eleventh hour to try to
win over their hearts and minds—well, he couldn't talk
in Vietnamese and they couldn't talk in American. Besides, to Calley it seemed that to tell everyone in Vietnam
your hearts and your minds, everyone—or your lives, was
to offer these people a Chinaman's choice. Be *circumcised*
or be beheaded—swell, that was an honest alternative,
but to offer to cleanse them of something so deep inside
them as to be quintessentially them, *We might as well
kill them,* Calley thought.

He killed them. He wasn't acting abnormally when
he killed them. His lips didn't froth when he told some
soldiers to waste them—he didn't scream, to Calley it
almost seemed that a voice outside of himself said the
word *waste* them and he, Calley, was nothing but a brass
instrument that it was trumpeted through. As one who

worked in the System, he had ridded himself of all such uncertain stuff as *I'd rather* and *I'd rather not*—of all except the infallible intellect, and he had been rolled by the natural laws of the universe to the only solution that got an infantry company to the China sea. It was simply inevitable and Calley couldn't alter it, Calley was just another wheel in the wheelworks of a size, a shape, and a suitable set of teeth to transmit the torque from the input to output end. To be integral with the machine was to rotate, willy-nilly, and to withdraw from it—well, really, to fit oneself in was nothing else but the American Way.

He was normal. The good doctor having said it, Calley got dressed in his brown tweed suit, put a bourbon into a black attaché case of Samsonite, got checked out of his hotel room in Manhattan, and flew economy class to Fort Benning, Georgia, the site of his small apartment and of his imminent trial. A duty would rest on Calley now that wouldn't if Calley were clinically crazy. A *normal* boy, it now would devolve upon him to offer himself to America as evidence of the innocence of all normal men —of all little wheels, of all whose consciences shared in a "Guilty" or "Not guilty." On trial, really, would be Calley's old company—one hundred men, of whom almost all had acquiesced to the unalterable and had killed civilians too. On trial would be Calley's own leaders, from the captain who—the night before—had told everyone to kill everything,

"Captain? Do you mean women and children, too?"

"I mean everything," to the full general who the next morning sent his CONGRATULATIONS. On trial in a court that a PFC may have hammered together of twopenny nails in plywood would be all normal men in America. Oyez. Oyez.

The inquiry began. At nine every day, the judge would come by the defense room to whistle, or clap three times, or reel an invisible fish in, or with his little finger out to ring an invisible dinner bell. "As we say in the infantry—"

"Here's how we do it," Calley would say, Calley's arm circling over him as though he were twirling a lasso—the infantry's sign for *assemble*.

"Mine is the casual one," the judge would say.

In the little defense room, an irrepressible sense of humor continued in Calley, a *joie de vivre* and a sense that as the approximate host in this sitting room he owed everyone a pleasant time. To the witnesses, he spoke of old times together in Tokyo or listened to their adventures in Georgia on twenty-five-dollar witness fees: in private homes where the women said, "I have beautiful breasts, don't I? Feel them," and private homes where the men insisted, "You can sleep here. You can sleep here. You—" *"What are you doing, man?"* He was always chipper with his Georgia friends.

"How things?"

"Oh, today they're trying to burn me."

Irrepressible—though no sooner was Calley in court itself than he changed into a stuffed specimen of Homo. The *élan vital* drained out of his eyes, nose, mouth, it was sucked to some inaccessible recess in Calley's intestines as this normal son of America let everyone see he was thoroughly what a component part of his country should be. A mechanical man, he sat at the defense's table like the Nixon at Disney World, in Florida, and the Turk that played chess with its wooden arm in Jackson's administration. Rivets attached each of Calley's feet to the courtroom floor—he didn't stir and his posture announced that he fitted into the System as squarely as any angle iron. His head didn't turn to its right or its left—if any emotion showed, it showed in the color of Calley's ears, an indiscreet organ that as the weeks went by the public came to watch carefully. It was as though in some factory loft the chevaliers du tastevin found a few unknown bottles of Tavel.

Of course, it was with regrets that the least inhibited man in Bangkok now chastened himself. He still loved life, but he recognized that to hop, skip, or jump through seventy years of his earthly incarnation was a life style that to his countrymen would be as abhorrent as to put wheat germ oil in Wonder bread. A man must whiten himself, it seemed to Calley. In fact, it was right here at officer candidate school that he had been taught to drop every unessential part of himself lest on the battle line he become the human equivalent to Caesar's impedimenta. To rise at exactly—*exactly*—five, to get dressed in clothes which only a CALLEY over the breast identified as not someone else's, to walk to his breakfast at the unalterable rate of two steps every second, the steps thirty inches apart—to exist this way, he had left spontaneity in his footlocker with his Canoe. The same in Vietnam—if anything, more, the people he killed wouldn't appreciate what a bar to efficiency life was if Calley had seemed to flaunt it, the same in the courtroom here. He sat still, he looked like the Pharaoh as week after week the troops testified against him. Name, address, occupation—

"How old are you?"

"Twenty-four."

"Are you married?"

"I am."

"Have you served in the Army?"

"I have."

"Do you know the accused?"

"I do."

"And would you point to him, please."

"Lieutenant William Calley."

"Let the record reflect that the witness pointed to—"

Calley just sat. On this twenty-first day of the case against him, he kept in control by remembering that— *if I get through today, I'm okay,* he meant it would be the defense's turn and he could sit in his oaken armchair till it turned into an antique without losing cool. But to-day, the last witnesses for the Army were on, the last temptations to Calley to give in to blushes, flushes, tears, to aspects that an American man was ashamed of. Calley sat stoically as the soldier now on the witness stand said he had served on that three-kilometer walk and he had watched as a hundred people—old men, women, and children—were led to the irrigation ditch of the village of Mylai.

"And—?"

"Calley was firing into the ditch."

"How long?"

"For approximately an hour."

A wax-museum man—Calley was still something on a circular stand at Madame Tussaud's. He didn't pale and he didn't let on that terror like a sudden hot shower had just taken over him. *An hour,* he was thinking, an hour would be time enough to kill everyone in a canyon—to fire forty thousand rounds, a minute's all he had really fired at the irrigation ditch. It was scary to Calley to hear someone lie, to Calley a lie of just thumbnail width was an irreversibly fatal one to his argument—to his life itself. He regarded it his defense that to die in that ditch inhered in the very destinies of the ten, twenty, whatever, the hundred people, that the incident lay at the end of a thread of inevitability that he—Calley—was just insane if he didn't acknowledge. To allow what was in fact automatic was to abase oneself to God, an omnipotence that he remembered would call for a massacre, sometimes,

Now go . . . and spare them not, but slay both man and woman, infant and suckling, ox and sheep, camel and ass.

to acquiesce in these acts of God or society could be scarcely something illegal. In his view, he had merely to let that thread of inevitability unroll and to pray every day it just wouldn't snap at anyone's lie. The truth, the whole truth, and nothing but the truth would set Calley free, Calley thought.

But this witness said, "An hour." A mad killer—this is what these words ostensibly made of Calley, he seemed like a man whose actions didn't flow out of mere surrender to necessity. He didn't have an eye that batted, though, though a look of great indignation showed on Calley's old lawyer as his cross-examination began.

"You were the team leader?"

"Yes."

"You went through the village?"

"Yes."

"Did you shoot anybody?"

"No."

A fishing trip, Calley knew. If the witness should lie, if the lawyer could trap him it would discredit him as other items had partly discredited the other eyewitnesses: a pervert, a peeping tom, and a GI who testified that on the fateful day, "I was emotional," "I was under emotional strain," "I got emotionally upset." But this witness, it was much slower going. A cold customer, he had never talked

to the lawyer in spite of his supplicatory telephone calls,
"He can get the death sentence. I know if I had that hanging over *me*—" "I don't want to." No success, the lawyer
for Calley knew nothing about this boy.

"The ditch. Did you ever see Sledge there?"

"I don't remember." A sob, a scream—a man couldn't
tell, as the witness spoke he bit on his lower lip to suppress
it. His feelings didn't show, and he testified with the cold
certitude of a plaintiff in a divorce case.

"Did you see Carter?"

"I don't remember."

"Did you see Dursi?"

"I don't remember."

"Did you see Cowan?"

"I don't remember."

"You have good eyesight, don't you?"

"Yes."

"You're not bothered by amnesia?"

"No."

Calley sat slumped in his wooden chair. The witness
was a Sahara, in his measureless sands the lawyer's words
were at once swallowed up and little survived but the
lie. In front of Calley the lawyer aged—a doddering man,
he was someone that a male nurse might take by the
elbow, helpfully.

A pause. "Did you throw grenades in the hooches?"

"No, I did not."

A pause. "Did you kill anybody in this operation?"

"No, I did not."

He played with a pointer. He stared at the scribbles the other three lawyers handed him—he didn't seem to fathom them, and he lowered them to the defense's table. "I think that's it," Calley's lawyer said.

"Why don't we recess," the judge suggested.

Exeunt all. In the defense room, the four defense lawyers met in a shapeless circle. A minute, an hour, a month—to the lawyers, the true duration of Calley's act didn't matter, murder is murder in Title Ten. But their bounden duty was to make wretched liars out of the other witnesses, regardless—to nullify them, and today success wasn't theirs. So they sulked, instead.

"He's petty."

"He hates him. It's obvious."

"He blurted that he was against the war."

"Well," Calley interrupted, and Calley now smiled again. "It could be worse."

A silence. The lawyers looked at Calley incredulously.

"We could go to the courtroom. And *kkk*," Calley went on. "They're making a gallows there. Or this little noose—"

"Well. We have to go for broke now," a lawyer said. "We can't say Bill didn't do it."

Calley smiled. It *would* be like lawyers to rest their case on the contention he hadn't done it—had been somewhere else, in Manila, in Miami at his poor grandmother's funeral, perhaps. At this trial, the mere testimony that he was seen somewhere east of Suez had been enough to get those lawyers to their feet to try every clever way to impeach it. Truth, Calley thought, was an unwelcome stranger here, "You lawyers," Calley would say. "A dead mule is lying right here and you say, 'It isn't dead.'" He himself would choose to admit it—a lie seemed to Calley to threaten the uninterrupted thread of inevitability if entered into the testimony by a defense witness, too. A few weeks from now, he meant to dispense with the fifth amendment and to testify that he had done it—had killed everyone at the irrigation ditch. Had even fired.

"We have to say, instead," the lawyer went on, "Bill was *ordered* to do it. The captain said to kill women and children."

"He didn't say it," Calley said.

"He didn't say it?"

"He didn't say it," Calley said. "He said to kill everyone."

"And that meant women and children, didn't it?"

"Sure. But he didn't say it."

"Bill," the lawyer protested. "If there is a village and if there's women and children there, if I say kill everyone did I say kill women and children?"

"No, you didn't."

"If there is this *house* and if there's women and children there, if I say kill everyone did I say kill women and children? If there is this baseball team—"

"I'm not going to lie about it."

"I'm not asking you to. If there is this woman, if I go—" the ruffled lawyer drew his finger across his throat—"if I do like this, am I saying kill her?"

"I'm not going to lie about it," Calley replied.

A difficult client. Of course, it wasn't that the lawyer had no respect for a man whose motto at every occasion seemed to be Veritas. To tell the truth worked, sometimes —on the witness stand, it was once invoked by a client of his who allegedly drove a getaway car, "I don't have a driver's license," "Not guilty." But the naked truth wouldn't work in Calley's case. To carry an Army rifle, to fire at some screaming men, at women, at children, to let their blood run in the irrigation ditch like in a roasting pan, to massacre them—to try, after that, to defend oneself by a mere recitation of what happened there at the ditch wasn't adequate. The lawyer's regrets to Calley, the doctrine of deaf inevitability wasn't in the common law or the jury's instructions.

Instead, the lawyer thought that a witness should tell the truth, sure, but *embellish* it. As it happened, in the defense room he practically had an infantry squad of GIs who quietly told him, "If there's anything I can say—" *I'll say it,* the boys intimated. Nor were these people untalented embellishers. One, a boy whose mustache recaptured those of the cardsharps on old riverboats, it seemed was a fugitive from a breach-of-promise suit. A girl wrote to Calley, "You better tell him to marry me. Or Daddy—" Another was a Negro boy whose goatee

moved like a steel rasp. A bad-looking cat, he told everyone that he did investigational work for California and
even demonstrated on Calley's girl.

"Is you been seeing a Mr. Calley?"

"Yes."

"Well, ma'am. He has a slight case of VD and—"

"Giggle."

"—and I'd like to inspect you. A *nurse* would like to
inspect you, a Caucasian nurse."

A third boy was not only ready to lie under oath but
at another trial in Georgia he *testified* so. All these would
be star witnesses, ways to lay shadows of reasonable doubt
on six honest officers—if Calley, if the client himself didn't
want it. Calley was almost puritanical about it. A typical
day, a witness was on and was starting on a tall story of
how someone felt up a VC nurse once. As always, the
lawyers were at it:

"I object!"

"I'm trying to show certain conduct by—" Calley's
lawyer replied. "Which, I think, has independent rele-
vancy to his state of mind and a direct bearing as to
whether he did issue orders on the fifteenth of—"

Blah blah blah. It was ended eventually by Calley,
who leaned across the defense's table to ask another
lawyer, "Is this necessary?"

"We'll talk about it."

"Is this completely necessary?"

He had that witness taken off. It wasn't that to Calley
a lie violated the boy-scout oath, a lie violated the inner

consistency of what every soldier did in Vietnam and of Calley's case, *I could hang for it,* Calley thought. It damaged him if the jury thought that to feel someone up or spontaneously think up some operational orders—to *choose* lay in any soldier's authority. The world simply turned—the sun rose inevitably, an act that would augur well for the robins though ill for the worms. A man just turned along with it—a captain, lieutenant, or PFC who had merely enrolled in the solar system might just as well acknowledge it, Calley believed. His lawyers demurred, his lawyers almost swooned on the afternoon that he itemized what he would testify to. His dress rehearsal in one lawyer's living room was a confession, nothing less.

"Excuse me, Bill," a lawyer said as Calley concluded, and he took another lawyer out on a dark veranda. "Is he really going to testify that he—"

"There's nothing that I can do. He insists."

The day came for Calley to vindicate himself in the courtroom. His shoes shined, he stood at attention, and he snapped into an "I do" as if it were right shoulder arms. He felt today like a man on the high palisades of Acapulco, *I'll give her a jump today, and if I miss*—it was better than to live fifty years knowing that he had done something so utterly loathsome that he had once lied to two hundred million people about it. For months, he had gone through his memory with a tweezer, almost, to recover every iota of his operation area and of his walk through it—Calley had even constructed a geographical model as big as a children's sandbox. "I'm hurting," Calley had often admitted to Georgia friends. "But when they get a picture of the combat operation—"

A real picture of this already was in the evidence and on the jury's inward eye. A photo of old men, women, and children strewn on the earth like the seaweed after a sea storm—a photo of twenty dead, it had been passed from one to another officer as though it had something slimy upon it. Studying it, a colonel chewed on his gray-rimmed glasses, a major made a Kabuki actor's grimaces, a major leaned over like one in a prayer stall, a major tapped with a Venus pencil, a major developed a knitted brow, and a captain whose face was like something they put on iodine bottles so people don't drink it evolved still more of a death's-head—it dropped on his chest like a severed head. In all, those officers served in Vietnam for six wartime years. A row of dead people—typical, and a doubt rested on these gentlemen that the photo needed a Calley to account for it. A major thought, *It could be a hoax.*

"Do you swear to tell the truth, the whole truth, and nothing but the truth?"

"Yes sir," Calley said.

His arm dropped. He went to his geographical model, he took up a wooden pointer, he stood like a pool player, waiting, impatiently tapping the pointer on his right foot. As the questions came, he told those jurors how he had straddled the irresistible impetus of circumstance until it had transported him to the irrigation ditch. At that time, he ordered the GIs, "Waste them."

"And what happened then?"
"I fired into the ditch also, sir."
"Did you look in the ditch?"
"Yes sir."
"And what did you see?"
"Dead people, sir."

THE VERDICT. *"It is my duty as president of this court to inform you that the court in closed session, and upon secret written ballot, two-thirds of the members concurring in each finding, finds you: of specification one of the charge, guilty of premeditated murder—"*
Calley fell backwards. The air pressure in his cheeks seemed to collapse—his lips became lines, his nose seemed to diminish in size, somehow, his eyes became round as a cornered rat's. Automatically, he saluted the colonel in whose avuncular voice (*"I'm sorry,"* it seemed to be telling him)—in whose voice the verdict of premeditated murder came, he kept silent but he licked a little invisible chalk from his lip. A few minutes later, he was taken away by MPs with supervisor armbands that he had once kidded about, "A supervisor! You get more money?" "No sir." He brought along a Gillette, but authorities at the post stockade wouldn't let in a shaving-cream bomb or the cellophane wrapper to Pall Malls, "You can make explosives with it." Nor would they let in Calley's Right Guard.
"Do you want to contact anyone?"

"Yes. President Nixon," Calley said.

He was smiling again—he was already breathing easy, he was satisfied with the verdict, to *be* on the highest authority a first-degree murderer was in fact healthier than to continue in existential anguish and in the empty exercise of *Who am I?* At last Calley knew—it was, after all, a corollary to his philosophy that the jury's decision would be definitive and he couldn't question it. Consider, the world to Calley was wheelworks, an interrelated system where he was supposed to clamp himself as securely as the last little oyster does in the Great Chain of Being. To the angels above—to the generals, to the experts in ultimate ends—he must entrust the solution to whether the great machine should go north, or three kilometers east, or south, or west, while whether or not this whole enterprise was a criminal one he entrusted to six good jurors, to the legitimate experts in Fact. On the august word of authority, he now understood what the system that he had once pledged his allegiance to had inevitably done in his eighteen months in Vietnam. It had perpetrated premeditated murder.

Ah so. It was perspicacious of Calley to see those criminal acts as inevitable ones. A system, remember, was something of wheels within wheels that to fit into flawlessly a man must become a wheel himself, forlorn of all that's alive. It didn't matter whether a system served what is ethically good or ethically evil—a war that's fought for God or some gremlin, an item that's supercolossal if swallowed once in the morning or, in fact, is always no better than the water inside it. A system didn't need a Nixon in charge—it didn't have to be misdirected, it could be a paradise but a man must *always* diminish to fit in its turbines and he must diminish down to the vanishing point to fit to a T. In systems, a fatal imperative prevailed: the more perfect the workings were, the more imperiled by the errors, inefficiencies, impurities, of the one unpredictable element. Man, as Eliot wrote, betrayed in the maze of his own ingenuities, condemned by the irrepressible presence of life, became an intolerable intrusion in his great apparatus. It had to cleanse him of cell after cell—it was never enough, a residue of the fortuitous remained and it ultimately had to murder him. We couldn't avert it, a row of dead bodies would be our inevitable legacy in Vietnam or anywhere one of our agents was. We had been wrong to think of Calley as not being normal—no, Calley was an American and what happened there at the irrigation ditch was the quintessential act of America. We were all William Calley.

SLAM. Calley thought, *It is so noisy here,* the stockade could be a rehearsal hall for a tropical steel band, it echoed every night to the steel against steel of doors, anvils, automobile fenders, kettles, lids, and a thousand thigh bones on aluminum gongs. At dawn every day, a hole in the wall shouted in Calley's cell, "Thirty minutes to mess," after thirty minutes it counted with all of the urgency of Mission Control, "Thirty seconds to—" "Twenty seconds to—" "Ten seconds to—" "Mess." In his military career, Calley had had his limbs slowly amputated until like a freak in some circus sideshow he now fitted into an area scarcely twelve feet by ten seconds wide. He still had his neck, however—the Army spared him a *coup de grâce* and it didn't eliminate the last several cells of life within him.

"It is my duty," the colonel said, in the courtroom again, "to inform you that the court in closed session, and upon secret written ballot, three-fourths of the members," etcetera, "sentences you to be confined at hard labor for the length of your natural life."

"I'll do my best, sir," Calley replied.

Roger. And right arm, a sharp salute told the colonel, the court, and the country that the mills of his gods couldn't grind him so wretchedly small that he still wouldn't continue to worship them. And turning, he walked down the courthouse stairs and he stepped out of history to the same inner sousaphones that he had entered to, a good soldier going to his *left,* right, *left*. He still was an Army officer, remember. A wheel within wheels, a man who didn't understand that in his very complicity with the System his criminality lay. It inhered in the verdict itself that to fit oneself into the Army or any great institution is to indenture oneself to a misanthropic master. In public, nations, in private, corporations, in all things, organizations, in the body itself the most tyrannous system there is, the omnipotent intellect—the ultimate need of a megamachine is the premeditated murder of its participants. To absent oneself is the only innocent act—to accept uncertainty, to trust oneself and to walk quietly out on the great dictator, the incontestable expert,